Toni Morrison's
BELOVED

CURRENTLY AVAILABLE

The Adventures of Huckleberry Finn
Mark Twain

Aeneid
Vergil

Animal Farm
George Orwell

The Autobiography of Malcolm X
Alex Haley & Malcolm X

Beowulf

**Billy Budd, Benito Cereno,
& Bartleby the Scrivener**
Herman Melville

Brave New World
Aldous Huxley

The Catcher in the Rye
J. D. Salinger

Crime and Punishment
Fyodor Dostoevsky

The Crucible
Arthur Miller

Death of a Salesman
Arthur Miller

The Divine Comedy (Inferno)
Dante

A Farewell to Arms
Ernest Hemingway

Frankenstein
Mary Shelley

The Grapes of Wrath
John Steinbeck

Great Expectations
Charles Dickens

The Great Gatsby
F. Scott Fitzgerald

Gulliver's Travels
Jonathan Swift

Hamlet
William Shakespeare

Heart of Darkness & The Secret Sharer
Joseph Conrad

Henry IV, Part One
William Shakespeare

I Know Why the Caged Bird Sings
Maya Angelou

Iliad
Homer

Invisible Man
Ralph Ellison

Jane Eyre
Charlotte Brontë

Julius Caesar
William Shakespeare

King Lear
William Shakespeare

Lord of the Flies
William Golding

Macbeth
William Shakespeare

A Midsummer Night's Dream
William Shakespeare

Moby-Dick
Herman Melville

Native Son
Richard Wright

Nineteen Eighty-Four
George Orwell

Odyssey
Homer

Oedipus Plays
Sophocles

Of Mice and Men
John Steinbeck

The Old Man and the Sea
Ernest Hemingway

Othello
William Shakespeare

Paradise Lost
John Milton

Pride and Prejudice
Jane Austen

The Red Badge of Courage
Stephen Crane

Romeo and Juliet
William Shakespeare

The Scarlet Letter
Nathaniel Hawthorne

Silas Marner
George Eliot

The Sun Also Rises
Ernest Hemingway

A Tale of Two Cities
Charles Dickens

Tess of the D'Urbervilles
Thomas Hardy

To Kill a Mockingbird
Harper Lee

Uncle Tom's Cabin
Harriet Beecher Stowe

Wuthering Heights
Emily Brontë

Toni Morrison's
BELOVED

Bloom's
NOTES

A CONTEMPORARY
LITERARY VIEWS BOOK

Edited and with an Introduction by
HAROLD BLOOM

Printed and bound in the United States of America.

First Printing
1 3 5 7 9 8 6 4 2

The hardback of this edition has been cataloged as follows:

Library of Congress Cataloging-in-Publication Data

Toni Morrison's Beloved / edited and with an introduction
by Harold Bloom.
  p.   cm. — (Bloom's notes)
  "A contemporary literary views book."
  Includes bibliographical references and index.
  ISBN 0-7910-4516-1 (hbk.) — ISBN 0-7910-5223-0 (pbk.)
  1. Morrison, Toni. Beloved.   2. Historical fiction, American—
History and criticism.   3. Afro-American women in literature.
  4. Infanticide in literature.   5. Slaves in literature.   6. Ohio—In
literature.   I. Bloom, Harold.   II. Series.
  PS3563.08749B4378   1999
  813'.54—dc21
                                              98-39619
                                              CIP

Chelsea House Publishers
1974 Sproul Road, Suite 400
Broomall, PA 19008-091

Contents

User's Guide

This volume is designed to present biographical, critical, and bibliographical information on the author and the work. Following Harold Bloom's editor's note and introduction are a detailed biography of the author, discussing major life events and important literary works. Then follows a thematic and structural analysis of the work, which traces significant themes, patterns, and motifs. An annotated list of characters supplies brief information on the chief characters in the work.

A selection of critical extracts, derived from previously published material by leading critics, then follows. The extracts consist of statements by the author, early reviews of the work, and later evaluations up to the present. These items are arranged chronologically by date of first publication. A bibliography of the author's writings (including a complete list of all books written, cowritten, edited, and translated), a list of additional books and articles on the author and the work, and an index of themes conclude the volume.

Harold Bloom is Sterling Professor of the Humanities at Yale University and Henry W. and Albert A. Berg Professor of English at the New York University Graduate School. He is the author of twenty books and the editor of more than thirty anthologies of literary criticism.

Professor Bloom's works include *Shelley's Mythmaking* (1959), *The Visionary Company* (1961), *Blake's Apocalypse* (1963), *Yeats* (1970), *A Map of Misreading* (1975), *Kabbalah and Criticism* (1975), and *Agon: Towards a Theory of Revisionism* (1982). *The Anxiety of Influence* (1973) sets forth Professor Bloom's provocative theory of the literary relationships between the great writers and their predecessors. His most recent books include *The American Religion* (1992), *The Western Canon* (1994), and *Omens of Millennium: The Gnosis of Angels, Dreams, and Resurrection* (1996).

Professor Bloom earned his Ph.D. from Yale University in 1955 and has served on the Yale faculty since then. He is a 1985 MacArthur Foundation Award recipient and served as the Charles Elkot Norton Professor of Poetry at Harvard University in 1987–88. He is currently the editor of other Chelsea House series in literary criticism, including MAJOR LITERARY CHARACTERS, MODERN CRITICAL VIEWS, and WOMEN WRITERS OF ENGLISH AND THEIR WORKS.

Editor's Note

My Introduction, somewhat at variance with the critical extracts, raises the question of ideological tendentiousness with regard to *Beloved*.

The critical views begin with the Canadian poet-novelist Margaret Atwood, for whom Morrison's "verbal authority" suffices. Roger Sale agrees, and finds *Beloved* to be "a long and beautiful tale."

Marilyn Sanders Mobley relates Morrison's novel to the slave narratives, as converting the memories of hatred into a communal mode of knowledge.

The exorcism of the ghostly Beloved is judged by David Lawrence to be a black self-purification, after which Bernard Bell praises the book's "black feminist sense of self-sufficiency."

Sethe's maternal crisis is examined by Stephanie A. Demetrakopoulos, while Linda Krumholz adds to the chorus of critics wholly persuaded by Morrison's mode of "rememory."

The murder of Beloved by Sethe is considered by Elizabeth Fox-Genovese "as a desperate act of self-definition," after which Ashraf H.D. Rushdy argues instead that slavery alone bears the guilt of this slaughter.

For Josef Pesch, *Beloved* has no closure, being a "post-apocalyptic" novel, while Caroline Rody rather differently sees the book as an ongoing history.

James Berger finds in *Beloved* an elegy for white liberalism in regard to race relations, after which Pamela E. Barnett concludes the critical extracts by fusing the images of rape and the supernatural in the novel.

Introduction

No dispute exists or ought to be fostered concerning Toni Morrison's strength as a literary artist. *Paradise* (1997) confirms yet once more her eminence at story-telling and as a prose stylist. Morrison herself has implied that the proper context for reading and studying her must be found primarily in African American women writers. On that view, Ralph Ellison is as unlikely a candidate for comparison as would be William Faulkner, Virginia Woolf, or Cormac McCarthy. And yet Toni Cade Bambara and Alice Walker do not help much in contextualizing Morrison. The most distinguished African American novel by any woman save Morrison is certainly Zora Neale Hurston's *Their Eyes Were Watching God,* a book totally remote from Morrison's mode and vision. Toni Morrison, like Faulkner and Cormac McCarthy, is a high rhetorician. Like Virginia Woolf, Morrison is a mythological and historical fantasist. *Beloved* purports to be a true history of African American slavery. The critic Stanley Crouch, disputing Morrison's version of history, rather unkindly termed *Beloved* a soap opera of the Black Holocaust. Few have agreed with Crouch; *Beloved* is central to the current canon of literature read and studied in American schools and colleges. I myself come neither to praise nor dispraise *Beloved,* but only to ask some questions about the book. Perhaps *Beloved* is a permanent work, perhaps not. In time, it may be regarded as a brilliant period piece, perfectly revelatory of the cultural age of Ideological Resentment, through which we continue to pass.

Beloved divides many of my acquaintances who possess critical discernment; for some of them it is a masterwork, for others it is supermarket literature. I myself am divided: no character in the novel persuades me, and yet much of this writing has authentic literary force. Few narratives since *Uncle Tom's Cabin* are as tendentious as *Beloved;* Morrison has a palpable design to impose upon her readers, and nothing in the book seems accidental or incidental. The novel is, to some extent, a punishment for black and white, male and female alike. The enormities of the horrors being represented give some authority to Morrison's moral judgments, implicit and explicit.

And yet there are virtually insurmountable aesthetic problems in the representation of any Holocaust, whether of six million Jews or of the "sixty million" African Americans to whom Morrison dedicates *Beloved*. Something in our psychic defenses is activated by a litany of atrocities that comprehends mammary rape, a mother's cutting of her baby's throat, whippings, dreadful prison treatment on chain gangs — I stop arbitrarily, rather than complete the catalog. However veiled by indirect style or supernatural intercessions, this profusion of torments may numb any reader's sensibilities. "Guilt is never to be doubted," the motto of Franz Kafka's penal colony, is not necessarily a formula for aesthetic achievement. Acknowledging culpability, at whatever level, itself can become an evasion of cognitive and aesthetic standards of judgment.

Since every critical view excerpted in this volume assumes the literary greatness of *Beloved*, I find myself the odd fellow out, but that may have some value for the student and the reader. In my own judgment, Morrison's authentic novels are *Sula* and *Song of Solomon*, the latter still her masterpiece. Morrison's prophetic and political vocation tends to make *Beloved* and *Jazz* somewhat problematic works for me. I conclude tentatively by noting again Morrison's remarkable ongoing gifts, that perhaps have found a better balance between ideology and story-telling in her recent *Paradise*. ✤

Biography of Toni Morrison

Toni Morrison was born Chloe Anthony Wofford on February 18, 1931, in the northern Ohio city of Lorain, the second of four children of George and Ramah Willis Wofford. Grandfather Willis had moved his family from Kentucky to Ohio in search of a better life; her father, a Georgia sharecropper, came north to work as a shipyard welder. Among the legacies from her family that influenced Morrison's life and writing are a strong, black self-image; examples of maternal authority and equality in marriage; and the power of black community. Although bitterly racist, George Wofford imparted to his daughter a strong sense of black identity. Ramah Wofford, counseling her daughter against crippling hatred, became a model for the powerful and resourceful women in Morrison's fiction. From her maternal grandparents, John Solomon and Ardelia Willis, Morrison heard stories of the post-Reconstruction South; from the black community's oral tradition Morrison heard terrifying and inspiring stories about black history and the Underground Railroad. About her roots as a writer, Morrison would later remark, "[T]he range of emotions and perceptions I have had access to as a black person and a female person are greater than those of people who are neither. . . . My world did not shrink because I was a black female writer. It just got bigger."

From early childhood Morrison was an accomplished storyteller and reader, expected to excel in school. She read widely in the works of English, French, and Russian novelists, and about the writings and accomplishments of African-Americans. In 1949 Morrison graduated from Lorain High School and entered Howard University, where she changed her name to Toni. As a member of the Howard Unity Players, the university repertory company, she toured the South. Graduating with a B.A. in English in 1953, Morrison enrolled at Cornell University, receiving an M.A. in English in 1955 for her thesis on the theme of suicide in the novels of William Faulkner and Virginia

Woolf. She taught English at Texas Southern University (1955–57) and at Howard University (1957–64). During her years at Howard she married Jamaican architect Harold Morrison, with whom she had two sons, Harold Ford Morrison, born in 1962, and Slade Kevin Morrison, born in 1965.

Divorced from her husband in 1964, Toni Morrison returned to Lorain with her children. By 1965 she had become an editor for a textbook subsidiary of Random House in Syracuse, New York. In 1967, she accepted a position at Random House in New York City and became a senior editor in 1968, a position she held until 1985. As senior editor, Morrison nurtured the talents of black writers such as Angela Davis and Toni Cade Bambara. *The Bluest Eye*, set in the African-American community in Lorain, Ohio, was published in 1969.

Morrison was Associate Professor of English at the State University of New York at Purchase in 1969, when she began work on her second novel. *Sula*, and an edition of Middleton Harris's *The Black Book*, were published in 1973. *Sula* was nominated for the 1975 National Book Award, received the Ohioana Book Award, and was featured as a Book-of-the-Month Club Alternate. While a visiting Lecturer at Yale University (1975–77), her third novel, *Song of Solomon,* was published; it received the National Book Critics Circle Award and the American Academy and Institute of Arts and Letters Award in 1977. *Tar Baby* was published in 1981. While a Schweitzer Professor of the Humanities at the State University of New York at Albany (1984–89), Morrison received the New York State Governor's Art Award (1986) and was a visiting lecturer at Bard College (1986–88). Her next novel, *Beloved,* was nominated for the 1987 National Book Award and the National Book Critics Award, and was awarded both the 1988 Pulitzer Prize for fiction and the Robert F. Kennedy Award. Morrison has suggested that *Beloved* and her 1992 novel, *Jazz,* constitute the first and second books in a planned trilogy. Her most recent novel, *Paradise,* was published in 1998.

In addition to literature, Morrison has written lyrics for Jessye Norman and collaborated with André Previn to write lyrics for songs sung by Kathleen Battle. She is a trustee of the National

Humanities Center, co-chair of the Schomburg Commission for the Preservation of Black Culture, and a member of the American Academy and Institute of Arts and Letters, the American Academy of Arts and Sciences, the National Council on the Arts, the Authors Guild, and the Authors League of America. She has received the Elizabeth Cady Stanton Award from the National Organization for Women and the 1993 Nobel Prize for Literature, as well as honorary degrees from Oberlin College, Dartmouth College, Bryn Mawr College, and Columbia and Yale Universities.

Since 1989 Morrison has been Robert F. Goheen Professor of the Humanities at Princeton University. ✤

Thematic and Structural Analysis

Book One, chapter i, introduces the motifs that will shape the major themes of Toni Morrison's *Beloved*. These include allusions to numerology and bestiality; the presence or absence of color; the natural world that may simultaneously reflect beauty and horror; the reciprocal bond between mother and child in breastfeeding and the mammary rape of Sethe; the iron that symbolically infuses Sethe's eyes and back with strength; the supernatural; and resurrection, both in the "dawn-colored stone studded with star chips" on Beloved's headstone and in the profane challenge of the murdered child's return to Sethe. Much of the narrative is in the form of flashback as the main characters remember past experiences.

The haunted house at 124 Bluestone Road, near Cincinnati, Ohio, is "spiteful" and "[f]ull of a baby's venom." In 1873, Sethe and her daughter, Denver, are all that remain of a once close family that included Grandma Baby Suggs; Sethe's two sons, Howard and Buglar; and her infant daughter, Beloved. Nine years earlier the boys had been driven away by the ghost of the dead Beloved and, shortly after, Grandma Baby Suggs died, "with no interest whatsoever in the boys' leave-taking or hers." Mother and daughter try, without success, to work a truce with this ghost who responds by moving the furniture.

Sethe's thoughts of the past revolve around her murdered child, Beloved, and ten minutes "rutting among the headstones with the engraver," his young son watching, "her knees wide open as any grave," as payment to have "Beloved" chiseled onto the marker. Now, she lives in a house "palsied by the baby's fury at having its throat cut." Baby Suggs once wryly remarked that Sethe should be thankful that she had three children alive—and only one "raising hell from the other side," since she had lost all eight of her own children. Sethe tries to remember as little as possible, but her brain is "devious." Memories of Sweet Home, the Kentucky farm where she and Halle and their children had been slaves, crowd her thoughts.

The abrupt arrival of Paul D Garner, a "Sweet Home Man," interrupts the solitude of Sethe and Denver. Sethe tells Paul D about the events that caused her to run from Sweet Home; about sending her sons and daughter north without her; about the white boys who stole her breast milk and then whipped her back raw; about the "whitegirl," who helped her survive and birth Denver; and about the death of her baby girl, Beloved. They talk about their life in slavery under the kindly Garners, the childless owners of Sweet Home, and the coming of the cruel overseer, known only as "schoolteacher," after the death of Mr. Garner. Sethe asks Paul D to stay. However, the ghostly light and sense of sorrow he feels from their house convince Paul D that Sethe and Denver should move out. Sethe replies, "I got a tree on my back and a haint [a ghost] in my house, and nothing in between but the daughter I am holding in my arms. . . . I will never run from another thing on this earth." Paul D massages Sethe's back, then strokes her breasts and Sethe begins to think that, perhaps, she could "[t]rust things and remember things because the last of the Sweet Home men was there to catch her if she sank."

Paul D violently drives the ghost from the house. But, with Paul D in her mother's bed and the ghost seemingly absent, Denver is lonely and apprehensive. She sits on the porch and "[s]lowly, methodically, miserably," eats bread and jelly.

Sethe and Paul D are both dissatisfied with their sexual encounter: "His dreaming of her had been too long and too long ago. Her deprivation had been not having any dreams of her own at all" (**chapter ii**). The tree on Sethe's back that "whitegirl" had likened to a chokecherry tree now seems to Paul D "a revolting clump of scars;" and her breasts he could "definitely live without." Sethe thinks that, after all, Paul D had done what one could expect of a man: He "ran her children out and tore up the house."

Sethe and Paul D lie quietly together, each with their own memories of slavery: Paul D of his slave-brother Sixo; Sethe of Mrs. Garner's kitchen, of her selection of Halle from among the male slaves and their six-year marriage, and of Halle's crippled mother, Baby Suggs, whom he worked for five years to emancipate. But Halle had been to Sethe more like a brother than a husband. Paul D thinks of his slave-brother Sixo arranging to meet Patsy the Thirty-Mile Woman, and of Sethe and her "marriage" to Halle. She naively had asked Mrs. Garner about a ceremony — "a preacher, some dancing, a party, a something" — and the woman had been amused, asking only if she were already pregnant. Sethe made a wedding dress of stolen scraps of material and Halle hung his "hitching rope" in her cabin. Sethe now recalls their coupling in the cornfield, announced to all by the movement of the cornstalks over their heads, while Paul D recalls enviously watching that very movement in the company of the other male slaves.

The novel's circular narrative draws also upon other impressions: "Denver's memories were sweet" (**chapter iii**), accompanied by the sensuous pleasure of cologne and the canopy of the boxwood hedge where, hidden and private, she may "stand all the way up in emerald light." Exhausted by loneliness, Denver retreats to this shelter to ponder the "magic" of her birth and the puzzle of Sethe's scant memories of her own mother, known only as Ma'am. The narrative voices of mother and daughter blend to retell the story of Sethe's ordeal after fleeing Sweet Home and of the cruel "schoolteacher." Saved from death by a sixteen-year-old indentured servant, Amy Denver, Sethe gave birth to Denver and the two women wrapped the baby in rags on the riverbank before Sethe escaped across the river into Ohio.

Meanwhile, inside the house Paul D sings prison songs as he repairs the broken furniture. He remembers "working like an ass" in the prison quarry and "living like a dog," but worse was "the box built into the ground" that had done him the favor of "[driving] him crazy so he would not lose his mind."

Sethe thinks of Denver, the focus of her life, a "charmed child" who "pulled a whitegirl out of the hill" to save them both, and who accompanied her mother to jail. Denver wants Paul D to leave, but Sethe wants him to stay. "As for Denver, the job Sethe had of keeping her from the past that was still waiting for her was all that mattered."

To ease the tension, Paul D takes them to a carnival (**chapter iv**). Images of violence and sensory confusion begin to shape the novel's tone: Roses die and their scent becomes "louder;" the white circus people astonish them by "eating glass, swallowing fire, spitting ribbons, twisted into knots, forming pyramids, playing with snakes and beating each other up." Illusions foreshadow the mystery about Beloved that Sethe will later reveal to Denver and Paul D. Late that afternoon Paul D, Sethe, and Denver return from the carnival to find a wet, exhausted woman resting in front of 124; she introduces herself as Beloved. As if newly born—or returning from the afterlife—she had crawled out of a stream and now rests against a mulberry tree, recalling Sethe's rest against the tree after Denver's birth. That Sethe does not see this young woman as any ghostly manifestation of her dead child suggests that the presence of this strange girl and the presence of the ghost are for Sethe separate, and contending, realities.

Images of infancy connect the visitor to Sethe's dead child: Her neck seems unable to support her head, her skin is soft and unlined, and she drinks as greedily as a nursing infant. Sethe's involuntary response upon seeing the girl is to lose control of her bladder, as if losing water before childbirth. Under Denver's watchful care, Beloved sleeps for four days in Baby Suggs's old room. Beloved is the "something" Denver has been waiting for to take away her loneliness.

Four weeks later (**chapter vi**) Beloved hovers like a "familiar" around Sethe, waiting for her when she returns from work and up before her every morning. Sethe is flattered by Beloved's devotion and answers her questions: "It became a way to feed her. Just as Denver discovers and relies on the delightful effect sweet things have on Beloved, Sethe learns the profound satisfaction Beloved gets from storytelling." But the retelling of these events hurts Sethe "like a tender place in the corner of her mouth that the bit left." A recurrent motif is in the power of human touch to heal and give comfort. Like Amy Denver massaging Sethe's feet, and Paul D touching Sethe's scarred back, Sethe grooms Denver's hair and answers Beloved's questions about her mother and the branding mark by which she was always to know her. As if an omen, a bit of Denver's hair thrown into the fire "explode[s] into stars" and Sethe, startled, recalls "something she had forgotten she knew." Her wet-nurse, Nan, had told Sethe stories in an African language she has forgotten: Sethe is the only child her mother, "taken up many times by the crew" on the slave ship, had not "thrown away." Denver is puzzled. How can Beloved know to ask her mother these most personal questions? Beloved reveals nothing about herself.

Paul D suspects that there is some significance to the timing of Beloved's arrival just when he, Sethe, and Denver have begun to feel like a family (**chapter vii**). At the very moment he decides to find another place for Beloved to live, she chokes violently on a raisin and Denver takes her to her room to rest. She now has a reason, at last, to claim Beloved as her closest companion. Paul D cannot understand why Sethe seems to hold on to Beloved. She tells him to "feel how it feels to be a colored woman roaming the roads with anything God made liable to jump on you." Paul D protests that he has "never mistreated a woman;" Sethe responds that Halle mistreated her by abandoning his children. Paul D reveals that Halle had been in the barn when the boys had taken Sethe's milk from her, and that it had broken him. In reaction he had scooped butter from a churn and smeared it on his face. Paul D, chained, with an iron bit in his mouth, could not comfort his friend. He never saw him again. Rage replaces Sethe's love for Halle as the memory fills her mind of "two boys with mossy teeth, one sucking on my breast the other holding me down, their book-reading teacher watching and writing it up," and Halle "looking and letting it happen." Paul D recalls his own humiliation under the gaze of the rooster, Mister, the proud witness to his degradation and the ruin of the Sweet Home men: "[W]asn't no way I'd ever be Paul D again, living or dead. Schoolteacher changed me. I was something else and that something was less than a chicken sitting in the sun on a tub." Sethe responds with soothing comfort, massaging his knee, her thoughts turning to her work kneading dough, at dawn, in Sawyer's restaurant kitchen: "Nothing better than that to start the day's serious work of beating back the past."

Denver craves a sisterly intimacy with Beloved and asks her, "What's it like over there, where you were before?" (**chapter viii**). Beloved describes a place that suggests both the womb and the grave — or Hell. She tells Denver she has "come back" only to be with Sethe, that "she left me behind. By myself." Denver responds by "construct[ing] out of the strings she had heard all her life a net to hold Beloved," telling her the story of her birth to the nineteen-year-old Sethe, then a year older than Denver is now. Denver, at last, sees her mother through Beloved. Her monologue becomes "a duet as they lay down together, Denver nursing Beloved's interest like a lover whose pleasure was to overfeed the loved." The narrative moves into Sethe's voice and we know details that Denver cannot. The contrasts between Sethe and Amy Denver are subsumed by their bond and knowledge as women on the riverbank: "They never expected to see each other again in this world and at the moment couldn't care less. But there on a summer night surrounded by bluefern they did something together appropriately and well. . . . wrapping a ten-minute old baby in the rags they wore." In this flashback Amy Denver resumes her quest to Boston for a piece of velvet, and Sethe, feverish from exhaustion and childbirth, prepares to cross the river to her children and Baby Suggs.

Religious conventions and the need for a ritual treatment of the past permeate **chapter ix**. The chapter tells how Baby Suggs ministered with Christlike intuition to her neighbors, urging children to laugh, men to dance, and women to cry. "She did not tell them to clean up their lives or to go and sin no more. She did not tell them they were the blessed of the earth, its inheriting meek or its glorybound pure. She told them that the only grace they could have was the grace they could imagine. That if they could not see it, they would not have it." Sethe's arrival, and learning from Baby Suggs about the presumed death of Halle, changes everything. "Those white things have taken all I had or dreamed," Sethe now recalls Baby Suggs saying. Relentlessly, "[h]er faith, her love, her imagination and her great big old heart began to collapse twenty-eight days after her daughter-in-law [Sethe] arrived."

Sethe, with Denver and Beloved, goes to the Clearing where Baby Suggs had ministered "to pay tribute to Halle, and to consider the idea of making a life with Paul D." She blames herself for Baby Suggs's death; she "knew the grief at 124 started when she jumped down off the wagon, her newborn tied to her chest in the underwear of a whitegirl looking for Boston."

Memory again returns Sethe to the riverbank where she waits, "alone and weak, but alive," with her baby, seeking a way to cross. She finds herself "near three coloredpeople fishing — two boys and an older man": Stamp Paid and his two sons. Stamp ferries Sethe and Denver across the Ohio River and hides them at a safe house (on the Underground Railroad). A young woman, Ella, brings news that Stamp had safely brought her three children to 124 Bluestone. Looking at Sethe's newborn child Ella muses that it's best not to love anything.

Sethe imagines the soothing touch of Baby Suggs' hands massaging her neck and is "actually more surprised than frightened to find that she was being strangled (**chapter ix**). Or so it seemed. Baby Suggs' fingers had a grip on her that would not let her breathe. Tumbling forward from her seat on the rock, she now claws at the hands that are there only in memory. Her feet are thrashing by the time Denver gets to her and then Beloved. Beloved then soothingly massages her neck and Sethe's "knotted, private, walk-on-water life gave in a bit," until she recognizes in Beloved's touch the presence of the baby ghost and breaks away.

Sethe is certain that she wants Paul D in her life. "Her story was bearable because it was his as well — to tell, to refine and tell again. The things neither knew about the other —the things neither had word-shapes to — well, it would come in time." Also in **chapter ix**, more details emerge about the death of baby Beloved and the response of the local black community. Denver recalls her brief education at Lady Jones' school that ended when a curious boy made clear to her why they were shunned: "Didn't your mother get locked away for murder? Wasn't you in there with her when she went?" Denver never returned to the school. Sethe observes that the crawling baby ghost became spiteful, her sons fled, and Baby Suggs died, all within twenty-eight days of her arrival with Denver at 124.

The journey of Paul D away from the horrific chain gang to freedom in the north (**chapter x**) was in sharp contrast to Sethe's journey. Hers was for reunion with her children; Paul D's was to put the past behind him. Sethe moved toward family, while Paul D moved toward an emotional hardness, until he was reunited with Sethe.

In **chapter xi**, however, Beloved gains emotional power over Paul D. She seduces him "with empty eye," promising to leave only if he will touch her "on the inside part" and call her by her name. Reality merges with dream as he reaches "the inside part" and awakens, calling out, "Red heart. Red heart. Red heart."

Denver is also seduced by Beloved (**chapter xii**). She imagines the attentions of a sister in the uncritical gaze of Beloved. Sethe occasionally questions Beloved about her past, but learns only that "she remembered a woman who was hers, and . . . being snatched away from her . . . [and] standing on a bridge looking down. And she knew one white man." Sethe concludes that Beloved had been abused and had "escaped to a bridge or someplace and rinsed the rest out of her mind." She thought this explained her apparent hatred for Paul D. Denver is certain that Beloved is 124's ghost and does not tell Sethe that Beloved and Paul D are lovers. Denver seeks only for ways to please Beloved and to keep her close. When she fears that Beloved has left, she cries "because she has no self" without her. Like an irritating small child, Beloved reappears, "standing where before there was nobody when Denver looked." Smiling, she "points to the sunlit cracks," telling Denver to look "over there. Her face." But Denver sees nothing.

Paul reflects on life under Mr. Garner at Sweet Home as Morrison deftly frames the paradox of benign slave ownership (**chapter xiii**): "He [Mr. Garner] thought what they [slaves] said had merit, and what they felt was serious. Deferring to his slaves' opinions did not deprive him of authority or power. It was schoolteacher who taught them otherwise. A truth that waved like a scarecrow in rye: they were only Sweet Home men at Sweet Home. One step off that ground and they were trespassers among the human race." Paul D tells Sethe that he has been overpowered by Beloved and, to reclaim Sethe, his manhood, and to escape Beloved's control, he suggests that they conceive a child. The power struggle between Paul D and Sethe intensifies.

In **chapter xiv**, Beloved reasserts her power over Sethe in a repulsive, infantile act: She pulls out a tooth with her thumb and forefinger. In an unusual revelation we know Beloved's thoughts. The pulled tooth, she thinks, presages her doom. She cannot remember "when she first knew that she could wake up any day and find herself in pieces. . . she thought it was starting." It is Beloved's only circumspect moment. Heavy winter snow heightens the isolation of the family as they move closer to the crisis foreshadowed by Beloved's thoughts of dismemberment.

In **chapter xv**, Baby Suggs, although dead, is brought back into the narrative to recall her joy over the arrival of Sethe's children, their reunion with Sethe, and her anguish over Halle. After Halle purchased her freedom, she had come, a free woman, to 124 Bluestone Road: "And it worked out, worked out just fine, until she got proud and let herself be overwhelmed by the sight of her daughter-in-law and Halle's children. . . . Now she stood in the garden smelling disapproval, feeling a dark and coming thing, and seeing high-topped shoes that she didn't like the look of at all."

Beloved, like a character from Greek tragedy, brings with her the retribution of the gods for Baby Suggs' imagined hubris (sin of pride). The chapter prepares us for the catalogue of the horrors of slavery described in **chapter xvi**.

Doom approaches fast as the "four [white] horsemen," symbols of the Apocalypse and signs of famine, war, pestilence, and death, arrive at 124 Bluestone (**chapter xvi**). In flashback, the dreaded schoolteacher, one of his nephews, one slave catcher, and a sheriff come to take Sethe — and her children — back into slavery. Sethe cuts the infant Beloved's throat and tries to kill her two sons and Denver to spare them that fate. As the sheriff takes Sethe into custody, she holds Denver to the nipple and the child swallows both milk and Beloved's shed blood. In a shocking juxtaposition, a white boy hands Baby Suggs a pair of shoes and demands they be repaired: "[Mama] says you got to have these fixed by Wednesday," and Baby

Suggs replies dully, "I beg you pardon. Lord, I beg you pardon. I sure do." (It is worth considering here the thoughts of writer Jamaica Kincaid, who recently asked how history might have been different if slaves had not embraced Christianity as their religion.)

Chapter xvii returns to the present as Paul D and Stamp Paid study a drawing from a newspaper, trying to discern if it is indeed Sethe who had been jailed for murdering Beloved. Paul D rejects the truth, arguing that "it's a mistake somewhere because that ain't her mouth." Sethe convinces him that the story Stamp tells is true (**chapter xviii**). "I stopped [schoolteacher]," she tells him, "I took and put my babies where they'd be safe." Paul D perceives that "[t]his here new Sethe didn't know where the world stopped and she began. . . . "Your love is too thick," he tells her. "Love is or it ain't," she replies, "Thin love ain't love at all." Proof that her love "worked" is that her children "ain't at Sweet Home. Schoolteacher ain't got em." Paul D leaves after harshly commenting, "You got two feet, Sethe, not four." Her act of murder may be somehow noble in these circumstances but, to Paul D, it also is bestial.

Book Two: chapter xix marks the shift in the reader's position from incomplete to complete knowledge of Sethe's act. Through the thoughts of Stamp Paid we follow the sequence of events culminating in the murder; he blames himself for Paul D's departure. Sethe recalls that "[t]hose twenty-eight happy days were followed by eighteen years of disapproval and a solitary life," until the arrival of Paul D.

In **chapter xx** Sethe remembers the past in short, explosive images. She claims Beloved as her daughter, returned "of her own free will and I don't have to explain a thing. . . . I'll explain to her, even though I don't have to. Why I did it. How if I hadn't killed her she would have died and that is something I could not bear to happen to her." She again recalls being forced to give up her child's milk, how "they held [her] down and took it."

Denver tells her story, as if to a biographer, in **chapter xxi**, beginning, "Beloved is my sister. I swallowed her blood right along with my mother's milk. . . . She was my secret company until Paul D came." Denver stays at home to protect Beloved from the harm she thinks Sethe will do, and waits in vain for her father, Halle, to return. Her happy memories of Baby Suggs have not been enough to sustain her, but the presence of Beloved is. Chapter xxii contains one certain statement by Beloved: "I am Beloved and she is mine." In the mind of the dead child come back to life sensory impressions yield images without logic or syntax, and they suggest her existence among the dead. She resists death only because of her love for Sethe, insisting, "I am not dead; I am not."

Chapter xxiii also begins "I am Beloved and she is mine." But, here, the language seems more earthly, and an interrogatory dialogue between mother and daughter merges with Denver's voice, revealing their mutual dependence as it reassures each of the others' devotion.

Chapter xxiv focuses upon Paul D as he relives the disintegration of Sweet Home after Mr. Garner's death: "Everything rested on Garner being alive. Without his life each of theirs fell to pieces. Now ain't that slavery or what is it?" The reality of slavery in the outside world had been unknown to them in that haven. Paul D was helpless in his humiliation as he and the others, Halle and Sixo, failed to escape. Only Sethe, he thinks, was strong enough to succeed. He respects and admires her courage, and accepts that she has greater monetary value as "property that reproduced itself without cost." Stamp Paid approaches Paul D to apologize and to offer lodging with any among the black community (chapter xxv). Paul D assures him that Reverend Pike has already made such an offer, but that he prefers to be alone. In Sethe's defense Stamp tells Paul D what he saw the day Sethe killed Beloved, declaring, "She ain't crazy. . . . She was trying to outhurt the hurter." Paul D asks, "How much is a nigger supposed to take?" to which Stamp stoically replies, "All he can."

In Book Three: chapter xxvi Sethe notices Beloved's neck scar and, from then on, "the two of them cut Denver out of the games: the cooking games, the sewing games, the hair and dressing-up games. Games her mother loved so well she took to going to work later and later each day" until she becomes obsessed with the tensions at 124 and loses her job. Beloved is a tyrant, taking "the best of everything," as Sethe cries and tells the unmoved child that "her plan was always that they would all be together on the other side, forever." All but Beloved are hungry and getting thinner. Sethe, losing her sanity, and Beloved, getting fatter by the day, are at war with each other. Denver turns to Lady Jones for maternal warmth and a job away from 124. Gifts of food from the women in the community begin to appear regularly. Denver tells Janey Wagon the story of 124, about Sethe's madness, and about her "cousin," Beloved. Janey knows that Beloved is a ghost and tells the women in the community. Edward Bodwin, the Quaker abolitionist who had provided the house for Baby Suggs and her family, hires Denver as a night nurse. He arrives in his cart at 124 and Sethe, in a flashback to the arrival of schoolteacher in a cart eighteen years earlier, runs at him with an ice pick. As Sethe runs toward Bodwin, Beloved watches him "rising from his place with a whip in his hand, the man without skin, looking. He is looking at her."

Here Boy, the family dog who disappeared when Beloved arrived, returns in **chapter xxvii** marking the departure of Beloved who "some say, exploded right before their eyes." Paul D is convinced that the reappearance of the dog is a sign that "124 is clear of her [Beloved]" and now, "[u]nloaded, 124 is just another weathered house needing repair. Quiet, just as Stamp Paid said." He finds Sethe in her room, talking incoherently to herself, and recalls Sixo describing his feelings for Thirty-Mile Woman: "She is a friend of my mind. She gather me, man. The pieces I am, she gather them and give them back to me in all the right order." Stamp Paid recalls how, despite the collar he had to wear, Sethe "never mentioned or looked at it," and so had "left him his manhood" on that last day at Sweet Home. "He wants to put his story next to hers." Sethe again becomes whole (**chapter xxviii**). Memories fade and they forget Beloved "like a bad dream." Beloved was reified ("thing-ified") anguish not containable by narrative; a living presence, a manifestation of Sethe's rage, of her helplessness, and of the insufficiency of mourning to remake the world. "This is not a story to pass on." But it is. ❖

List of Characters

Sethe (b.1835) is a survivor of slavery. At age 13, she is brought to Sweet Home, an idyllic Kentucky plantation owned by the kindly Garners. Within a year, she has chosen Halle as her "husband" and, by age 18, has born three children. When a brutal overseer takes charge, Halle and the rest of the "Sweet Home men" attempt to escape, and Sethe sends her children to Ohio on the Underground Railroad, planning to follow them later. The bitter memory of boys holding her down and taking her breast milk; the brutal lashing afterward; her flight and Denver's birth; all is soothed by Baby Suggs when Sethe at last reaches Cincinnati. When the overseer comes to reclaim her and her children under the Fugitive Slave law, Sethe cuts the throat of her oldest daughter and attempts to kill the others, and is condemned to hang. She gains release and returns to the house at 124 Bluestone Road. After the death of Baby Suggs, she lives in solitude with Denver and the ghost of her murdered infant daughter, Beloved. The arrival of Paul D eighteen years later presages the ghost's departure and Sethe's emotional healing as their narratives interweave and they make their stories one.

Beloved (1854–1855) is Sethe's infant daughter and Denver's older sister, murdered by Sethe to spare her from slavery. She is the venomous baby, the "almost crawling? baby," and the Beloved of the title. She haunts 124 Bluestone Road as a spirit and as a young woman who clings to Sethe like a vengeful familiar, seduces Paul D, and manipulates Denver. Beloved is reified (thing-ified) anguish not containable by Sethe's narrative, a living presence, a manifestation of Sethe's rage and helplessness.

Denver (b.1855) is Sethe's 18-year-old daughter. Solitary and imaginative, she clings to the preternatural and malicious Beloved as a sister and companion. Born during Sethe's flight from Sweet Home to Cincinnati, she survives the scene of Beloved's murder and becomes the focus of Sethe's life. Sethe thinks of her as "a charmed child" who "pulled the white girl [Amy Denver] out of the hill" to save them both." As the first African-American generation born out of slavery she can make a place for herself in the world in a way that her mother cannot—whether it be a hiding place in the hedge, in her room with her sister, Beloved, at Lady Jones' school, or among the community of women who move to help her and Sethe in their crisis.

Howard (b.1850) and *Buglar* (b.1851) are Sethe's sons. They run away from 124 Bluestone Road, the haunting by the baby ghost too terrifying for them to endure.

Paul D Garner is a "Sweet Home man," and a compassionate and empathetic lover who helps Sethe to survive the demands of Beloved and to live with memories of slavery. He has been harnessed like livestock, a bit in his mouth; he sings songs learned on a Georgia chain gang after his attempted escape from Sweet Home; he has known helplessness and humiliation as powerful as Sethe's. Considering his brutal history, he is a remarkably, almost unbelievably, good man.

Halle Suggs (b.1835–1855) is the father of Sethe's children, and the youngest of Baby Suggs' eight children. He works for five years to purchase freedom for his mother, who moves to Cincinnati and the house at 124 Bluestone Road. He disappears after the escape from Sweet Home, broken by the sight of Sethe's degradation by the schoolteacher and his nephews.

Baby Suggs (Grandma Baby) (1795–1865) is the mother of Halle. In Cincinnati she becomes a spiritual leader in the black community, ministering to men, women, and children, urging them to recognize themselves as loving beings, not brutalized slaves. She dies twenty-eight days after Sethe's arrival with Denver at 124 Bluestone.

Stamp Paid (Joshua) is the Kentucky slave who ferries Sethe and Denver across the Ohio River. Earlier, he had delivered her three children to Grandma Baby's house. When Sethe tries to kill her children, he saves Denver.

Amy Denver is the sixteen-year-old, white indentured servant running away to Boston on a quest for "a piece of velvet." She finds Sethe, her feet too swollen to walk, able only to crawl to a nearby shed. Amy massages her feet and soothes Sethe's festering back, likening the forming scars to a chokecherry tree. She helps Sethe in childbirth, then continues her journey, asking that Sethe tell the baby her name.

Mr. Garner is the benign master of Sweet Home. His death leaves the plantation in debt and forces Mrs. Garner to sell their slaves. That he treated his slaves well makes no difference in the fates of the "Sweet Home men" and Sethe, proof that slavery could never be anything but inhumane.

Mrs. Lillian Garner is the wife of Mr. Garner. She is kind to Sethe, but amused when the young girl asks about a ceremony to mark her wedding to Halle. Slaves have no weddings, but she gives Sethe a pair of crystal earrings to mark the occasion. After her husband's death she sells Paul D to settle debts and makes "schoolteacher" overseer.

Schoolteacher is the widowed brother-in-law of Mr. Garner. He foils the escape attempts of the Sweet Home men; observes and coldly records the taking of Sethe's milk by his two nephews; and comes to capture Sethe and her children in Cincinnati. For him, slaves are farm stock and Sethe is valuable as a breeder of new slaves.

Sixo is burned alive by schoolteacher after attempting to escape Sweet Home. As he dies, he sings for his unborn child, "Seven-O! Seven-O!"

Patsy, the Thirty-Mile Woman, carries Sixo's child. She joins the escape from Sweet Home and watches from her hiding place as schoolteacher and his men capture Sixo and Paul D.

Paul A Garner, a Sweet Home man. After he is caught in the escape, tortured, and killed, his "headless, feetless torso" hangs from a tree as proof of his worthlessness.

Paul F Garner, a Sweet Home man, sold by Mrs. Garner to pay plantation debts.

Ma'am is Sethe's mother, a field hand recognizable only by her hat. She reveals to Sethe a tattoo under her breast, a mark by which Sethe may identify her as her mother. When Ma'am is later hanged for some unknown offense, her corpse is too mutilated for Sethe to recognize. On the slave ship from Africa she bears Sethe, the only of her offspring she does not abort or kill, the child of the one man whom she loved.

Nan is the plantation wet-nurse who was brought from Africa on the same slave ship as Ma'am. She tells Sethe the story of her birth and that she is named for her father.

Ella is a conductor on the Underground Railroad who escorts Sethe and the infant Denver to 124 Bluestone Road. A slave herself, she brings food and clothing to Sethe and the infant Denver. She observes, "If anybody was to ask me I'd say, 'Don't love nothing.'"

Lady Jones is the light-skinned teacher who conducts classes in her home for the "unpicked children of Cincinnati." She finds Denver a job, offers her education, and instinctively responds to her emotional need.

Edward Bodwin is a Quaker abolitionist and supporter of the Underground Railroad. His home is a way station, yet he keeps on a shelf a small figurine of a slave on his knees. He secures Sethe's release after her imprisonment.✤

Critical Views

[Margaret Atwood is one of Canada's most distinguished novelists, poets, and literary critics. Her critical
works include *Survival: A Thematic Guide to Canadian
Literature* (1972) and *Second Words: Selected Critical
Prose* (1982). Among her many novels are *The Hand-
maid's Tale* (1986), *Cat's Eye* (1989), *The Robber Bride*
(1993), and *Alias Grace* (1996). In this extract, Atwood
describes the ways in which memory becomes nightmare, and how magic at last heals Sethe, Denver, and
Paul D.]

Through the different voices and memories of the book,
including that of Sethe's mother, a survivor of the infamous
slave-ship crossing, we experience American slavery as it was
lived by those who were its objects of exchange, both at its
best—which wasn't very good—and at its worst, which was as
bad as can be imagined. Above all, it is seen as one of the
most viciously antifamily institutions human beings have ever
devised. The slaves are motherless, fatherless, deprived of their
mates, their children, their kin. It is a world in which people
suddenly vanish and are never seen again, not through acci-
dent or covert operation or terrorism, but as a matter of
everyday legal policy.

   Slavery is also presented to us as a paradigm of how most
people behave when they are given absolute power over other
people. The first effect, of course, is that they start believing in
their own superiority and justifying their actions by it. The
second effect is that they make a cult of the inferiority of those
they subjugate. It's no coincidence that the first of the deadly
sins, from which all the others were supposed to stem, is Pride,
a sin of which Sethe is, incidentally, also accused.

In a novel that abounds in black bodies—headless, hanging from trees, frying to a crisp, locked in woodsheds for purposes of rape, or floating downstream drowned—it isn't surprising that the "whitepeople," especially the men, don't come off too well. Horrified black children see whites as men "without skin." Sethe thinks of them as having "mossy teeth" and is ready, if necessary, to bite off their faces, and worse, to avoid further mossy-toothed outrages. There are a few whites who behave with something approaching decency. There's Amy, the young runaway indentured servant who helps Sethe in childbirth during her flight to freedom, and incidentally reminds the reader that the nineteenth century, with its child labor, wage slavery and widespread and accepted domestic violence, wasn't tough only for blacks, but for all but the most privileged whites as well. There are also the abolitionists who help Baby Suggs find a house and a job after she is freed. But even the decency of these "good" whitepeople has a grudging side to it, and even they have trouble seeing the people they are helping as full-fledged people, though to show them as totally free of their xenophobia and sense of superiority might well have been anachronistic.

Toni Morrison is careful not to make all the whites awful and all the blacks wonderful. Sethe's black neighbors, for instance, have their own envy and scapegoating tendencies to answer for, and Paul D., though much kinder than, for instance, the woman-bashers of Alice Walker's novel *The Color Purple*, has his own limitations and flaws. But then, considering what he's been through, it's a wonder he isn't a mass murderer. If anything, he's a little too huggable, under the circumstances.

Back in the present tense, in chapter one, Paul D. and Sethe make an attempt to establish a "real" family, whereupon the baby ghost, feeling excluded, goes berserk, but is driven out by Paul D.'s stronger will. So it appears. But then, along comes a strange, beautiful, real flesh-and-blood young woman, about twenty years old, who can't seem to remember where she comes from, who talks like a young child, who has an odd, raspy voice and who says her name is Beloved.

Students of the supernatural will admire the way this twist is handled. Ms. Morrison blends a knowledge of folklore—for instance, in many traditions, the dead cannot return from the grave unless called, and it's the passions of the living that keep them alive—with a highly original treatment. The reader is kept guessing; there's a lot more to Beloved than any one character can see, and she manages to be many things to several people. She is a catalyst for revelations as well as self-revelations; through her we come to know not only how, but why, the original child Beloved was killed. And through her also Sethe achieves, finally, her own form of self-exorcism, her own self-accepting peace.

Beloved is written in an antiminimalist prose that is by turns rich, graceful, eccentric, rough, lyrical, sinuous, colloquial and very much to the point. Here, for instance, is Sethe remembering Sweet Home:

> ...suddenly there was Sweet Home rolling, rolling, rolling out before her eyes, and although there was not a leaf on that farm that did not want to make her scream, it rolled itself out before her in shameless beauty. It never looked as terrible as it was and it made her wonder if hell was a pretty place too. Fire and brimstone all right, but hidden in lacy groves. Boys hanging from the most beautiful sycamores in the world. It shamed her—remembering the wonderful soughing trees rather than the boys. Try as she might to make it otherwise, the sycamores beat out the children every time and she could not forgive her memory for that.

In this book, the other world exists and magic works, and the prose is up to it. If you can believe page one—and Ms. Morrison's verbal authority compels belief—you're hooked on the rest of the book.

The epigraph to *Beloved* is from the Bible, Romans 9:25: "I will call them my people, which were not my people; and her beloved, which was not beloved." Taken by itself, this might seem to favor doubt about, for instance the extent to which Beloved was really loved, or the extent to which Sethe herself was rejected by her own community. But there is more to it than that. The passage is from a chapter in which the Apostle Paul ponders, Job-like, the ways of God toward humanity, in particular the evils and inequities visible everywhere on the earth. Paul goes on to talk about the fact that the Gentiles, hitherto despised and outcast, have now been redefined as acceptable. The passage proclaims, not rejection, but reconciliation and hope. It continues: "And it shall come to pass, that in the place where it was said unto them, Ye are not my people; there shall they be called the children of the living God."

Toni Morrison is too smart, and too much of a writer, not to have intended this context. Here, if anywhere, is her own comment on the goings-on in her novel, her final response to the measuring and dividing and excluding "schoolteachers" of this world. An epigraph to a book is like a key signature in music, and *Beloved* is written in major.

—Margaret Atwood, "Haunted by Their Nightmares," *The New York Times Book Review* (September 13, 1987): 45–47.

❖

ROGER SALE ON STORYTELLING AS REMEMORY IN *BELOVED*

[Roger Sale teaches in the Department of English at the University of Washington, Seattle. His works include *Modern Heroism: Essays on D.H. Lawrence, William Empson, and J.R.R. Tolkien* (1973), *Literary Inheritance* (1984), and *Closer to Home: Writers and Places in England, 1780–1830* (1986). In this extract, Sale points out the unique structure of *Beloved* as story, elegy, and rememory.]

It is Toni Morrison's ambition to create a form, and a storytelling, that keeps alive the struggle to remember, the need to forget, and the inability to forget. Something terrible happened, and keeps happening, and it is not entirely clear what, or even when. Though the events of *Beloved* could be arranged to make a drama, though there is a grand climatic scene, the book is elegy, pastoral, sad, sweet, mysterious.

I trace part of a thread: way back, about as far back as the novel's memory goes, a slave named Halle got permission from his owner to work for pay on Sundays so that, years later, after Halle had married Sethe, he could buy freedom for his mother, Baby Suggs. With the help of the whites who own the house, Baby Suggs had come to live at 124—so that 124 is where Halle and Sethe will come after they escape, except they are separated and Sethe arrives alone. Baby Suggs had "decided that, because slave life had 'busted her legs, back, head, eyes, hands, kidneys, womb and tongue,' she had nothing left to make a living with but her heart," and she becomes a preacher:

> The company watched her from the trees. They knew she was ready when she put her stick down. Then she shouted, "Let the children come!" and they ran from the trees toward her.
>
> "Let your mothers hear you laugh," she told them, and the woods rang. The adults looked on and could not help smiling.
>
> Then "Let grown men come," she shouted. They stepped out one by one among the ringing trees.
>
> "Let your wives and children see you dance," she told them, and groundlife shuddered under their feet.
>
> Finally, she called the women to her. "Cry," she told them.
>
> "For the living and the dead. Just cry." And without covering their eyes the women let loose.
>
> It started that way: laughing children, dancing men, crying women and then it got mixed up. Women stopped crying and danced; men sat down and cried; children danced, women laughed, children cried until, exhausted and riven, all and each lay about the Clearing damp and gasping for breath, In the silence that followed, Baby Suggs, holy, offered up to them her great big heart.

But this rememory, called up because Paul D's arrival, which killed the ghost, forced Sethe to tell herself she would never see Halle again: "Why now, with Paul D instead of the ghost, was she breaking up? Getting scared? Needing Baby? The worst was over, wasn't it?"

No, because other parts of the past can reach out and clutch like the tentacles of an octopus, because Beloved is there to cast a spell over Sethe, because Denver must finally seize the day, because Paul D, who had locked the tobacco tin of his past in his chest must come to remember. Yet there does come a time when the worst indeed is over:

> "Seth," Paul D says, "me and you, we got more yesterday than anybody. We need some kind of tomorrow."

> He leans over and takes her hand. With the other he touches her face. "You your best thing, Sethe. You are." His holding fingers are holding hers.

> "Me? Me?"

Paul D is strong here because he has remembered what another slave had said, twenty years ago, about his woman, "She is a friend of my mind," and so Paul D can know what Sethe is for him. And she, bewildered, loved, can now forget. It's a long and beautiful tale.

> —Roger Sale, "Toni Morrison's *Beloved*" (originally "American Novels, 1988"), *Massachusetts Review* 29:1 (Spring 1988): 81–86.

♣

MARILYN SANDERS MOBLEY ON THE CALL AND RESPONSE PATTERN IN *BELOVED*

[Marilyn Sanders Mobley is Assistant Professor of English at George Mason University. She has written essays on Morrison, Sarah Orne Jewett, Ann Petty, Zora Neal Hurston. She is currently at work on a study of narrative poetics in Morrison's novels. In this extract, Mobley focuses upon the African-American oral tradition, the structure of the narratives of Sethe, Paul D, Baby Suggs, Denver, and *Beloved*.]

While all texts develop to a certain extent by secrecy or by what information they withhold and gradually release to the reader, the text of *Beloved* moves through a series of narrative starts and stops that are complicated by Sethe's desire to forget or "disremember" the past. Thus, at the same time that the reader seeks to know "the how and why" of Sethe's infanticide, Sethe seeks to withhold that information not only from everyone else, but even from herself. Thus, the early sections of the novel reveal the complex ways in which memories of the past disrupt Sethe's concerted attempt to forget.

The first sign of this tension between remembering and forgetting occurs on the second page of the text in a scene where Denver and Sethe attempt to call the ghost forth. When Denver grows impatient with the seeming reluctance of the ghost to make its presence felt, Sethe cautions her by saying: "You forgetting how little it is . . . She wasn't even two years old when she died." Denver's expression of surprise that a baby can throw such a "powerful spell" is countered in the following passage:

> 'No more powerful than the way I loved her,' Sethe answered and there it was again. The welcoming cool of unchiseled headstones; the one she selected to lean against on tiptoe, her knees wide open as any grave. Pink as a fingernail it was, and sprinkled with glittering chips...Counting on the stillness of her own soul, she had forgotten the other one: the soul of her baby girl.

In this passage we have several things occurring at once. First, Sethe's verbalization of love triggers her memory of selecting a tombstone for the baby she murdered. The phrase "there it was again" signals that this is a memory that recurs and that brings the ambivalent emotions of consolation and anguish. Second, the memory of the tombstone triggers her memory of the shameful circumstances of getting it engraved. In this memory, the reality of gender and oppression converge, for the engraver offers to place seven letters— the name "Beloved"—on the headstone in exchange for sex. She also remembers that for ten more minutes, she could have gotten the word "dearly" added. Thirdly, this memory raises the issue around which the entire novel is constructed and which is the consequence and/or responsibility that she must carry for her actions.

Throughout the novel there are similar passages that signal the narrative tension between remembering and forgetting. At various points in the text, a single phrase, a look or the most trivial incident rivets Sethe's attention to the very details of the past she is least ready to confront. In the words of the text, "she worked hard to remember as close to nothing as was safe." In another place the text refers to the "serious work of beating back the past." Moreover, a mindless task such as folding clothes takes on grave significance, as the following passage suggests: "She had to do something with her hands because she was remembering something she had forgotten she knew. Something privately shameful that had seeped into a slit in her mind." Morrison even includes vernacular versions of words to suggest the slaves' own preoccupation with mnemonic processes. For example, at one point "rememory" is used as a noun, when Sethe refers to what Paul D stirs up with his romantic attention to her. Later, the same word is used as a verb, when Sethe begins to come to terms with the past through her relationship with Beloved. She allows her mind to be "busy with the things she could forget" and thinks to herself: "Thank God I don't have to rememory or say a thing." Even the vernacular word for forgetting, "disremember," calls our attention to its binary opposite of remembering.

When Paul D arrives at Sethe's home on 124 Bluestone, Denver seeks to frighten this unwanted guest away by telling him they have a "lonely and rebuked" ghost on the premises. The obsolete meaning of rebuked—repressed—not only suggests that the ghost represents repressed memory, but that, as with anything that is repressed, it eventually resurfaces or returns in one form or another. Paul D's arrival is a return of sorts in that he is reunited with Sethe, his friend from Mr. Garner's Sweet Home plantation. His presence signals an opportunity to share both the positive and negative memories of life there. On the one hand, he and Sethe talk fondly of the "headless bride back behind Sweet Home: and thus share a harmless ghost story of a haunted house. On the other hand, when they remember Sweet Home as a place, they regard it with ambivalence and admit that "it wasn't sweet and it sure wasn't home."

What also comes back through the stories Paul D shares are fragments of history Sethe is unprepared for such as the fact that years ago her husband had witnessed the white boys forcibly take milk from her breasts, but had been powerless to come to her rescue or stop them. Furthermore, his personal stories of enduring a "bit" in his mouth—the barbaric symbol of silence and oppression that Morrison says created a perfect "labor force"—along with numerous other atrocities, such as working on the chain gang, introduce elements of the classic slave narrative into the text. Perhaps more importantly, these elements comprise the signs of history that punctuate the text and that disrupt the text of the mind which is both historical and ahistorical at the same time.

I believe the meaning of Morrison's complex use of the trope of memory becomes most clear in what many readers regard as the most poetic passages in the text. These passages appear in sections two through five of Part Two, where we have a series of interior monologues that become a dialogue among the three central female characters. The first is Sethe's, the second is Denver's, the third is Beloved's and the last one is a merging of all three. Beloved's is the most intriguing, for the text of her monologue contains no punctuation. Instead, there are literal spaces between groups of words that signal the time-lessness of her presence as well as the unlived spaces of her life. Earlier in the novel, Sethe even refers to Beloved as "her daughter [who had] . . . come back home from the timeless place." Samples of phrases from Beloved's monologue reveal the meaning of her presence: "[H]ow can I say things that are pictures I am not separate from her there is no place where I stop her face is my own . . . all of it is now it is always now." These words suggest not only the seamlessness of time, but the inextricability of the past and present, of ancestors and their progeny. In the last interior "dialogue," the voices of Sethe, Denver and Beloved blend to suggest not only that it is always now, but to suggest that the past, present and future are all one and the same.

In an article entitled "Rediscovering Black History," written on the occasion of the publication of the *The Black Book*, Toni Morrison speaks of the "complicated psychic power one had to exercise to resist devastation." She was speaking, of course, not just of slavery, but of the Black existence in America after slavery as well. *Beloved* and all her novels, to a certain extent, bear witness to this psychic power. It must be stated as I conclude, however, that my intertextual reading of this novel as a revision of the slave narrative should not be construed as an attempt to diminish the form and content of the slave narratives themselves in any way. It is, instead, a recognition of the truth that Gates offers in the introduction to *The Slave's Narrative:*

> Once slavery was abolished, no need existed for the slave to write himself [or herself] into the human community through the action of first-person narration. As Frederick Douglass in 1855 succinctly put the matter, the free human being "cannot see things in the same light with the slave, because he does not and cannot look from the same point from which the slave does" . . . The nature of the narratives, and their rhetorical strategies and import, changed once slavery no longer existed.

Beloved is a complex, contemporary manifestation of this shift. In a larger sense, however, it is what Mikhail Bakhtin calls a "reaccentuation" of the past (in this case, the past of slavery) to discover newer aspects of meaning embedded in the classic slave narrative. Morrison's purpose is not to convince white readers of the slave's humanity, but to address black readers by inviting us to return to the very part of our past that many have repressed, forgotten or ignored. At the end of the novel, after the community has helped Denver rescue her mother from Beloved's ferocious spell by driving her out of town, Paul D returns to Sethe "to put his story next to hers." Despite the psychic healing that Sethe undergoes, however, the community's response to her healing is encoded in the choruslike declaration on the last two pages of the text, that this was "not a story to pass on." Yet, as readers, if we understand Toni Morrison's ironic and subversive vision at all, we know that our response to the text's apparent final call for silence and forgetting is not that at all. Instead, it is an ironic reminder that the process of consciously remembering not only empowers us to tell the difficult stories that must be passed on, but it also empowers us to make meaning of our individual and collective lives as well.

—Marilyn Sanders Mobley, "A Different Remembering: Memory, History and Meaning in Toni Morrison's *Beloved*," *Modern Critical Views: Toni Morrison*, edited by Harold Bloom. (New York: Chelsea House, 1988). ✤

[Susan Bowers is co-editor of *Gender, Culture, and the
Arts: Women, the Arts, and Society* (1993), *Politics,
Gender, and the Arts* (1992), and *Sexuality, the Female
Gaze, and the Arts* (1992). In this extract, Bowers shows
how Morrison compels readers to imaginatively live the
experience of slavery and transform it into new narratives of African-American community.]

Morrison shares with post-Holocaust Jewish artists the monu-
mental difficulties attendant of depicting the victims of racial
genocide. What Elie Weisel has stated about the Holocaust
applies to the slaughter of ten times as many Africans and
African-Americans as the six million Jews killed by Hitler (Morrison has said that 60 million is the smallest figure she had
gotten from anyone for the number of slaves who died as a
result of slavery.

> The Holocaust is not a subject like all the others. It imposes certain
> limits . . . In order not to betray the dead and humiliate the living,
> this particular subject demands a special sensibility, a different
> approach, a rigor strengthened by respect and reverence and,
> above all, faithfulness to memory.

Betrayal would include sentimentalizing and thus trivializing
the victims of slavery, rendering them merely pathetic and
pitiable. Morrison does not do that. She dedicated *Beloved* to
the "Sixty Million and More," and her novel conjures slaves
back to life in many-dimensional characters with a full range of
human emotions. They love and hate, sin and forgive, are
heroic and mean, self-sacrificing and demanding. They endure
incredible hardships to sustain relationships, but the inconceiv-
able brutality and degradation which they experience fractures
their communities and inflicts both physical and perhaps
irreparable psychological damage on individuals.

One of the questions which *Beloved* asks is whether it is possible to transform unspeakably horrific experiences into knowledge. Is the magnitude of their horror too great to assimilate? Perhaps because the novel asks its readers, especially African-Americans, to "dwell on the horror" which those rushing away from slavery could not, it addresses what happens when the magnitude of that horror is acknowledged, even suggesting how to survive the bringing into consciousness of what has lain hidden for so long. The struggle of *Beloved*'s characters to confront the effects of the brutality and to recover their human dignity, their selves "dirtied" by White oppression—to transform their experiences into knowledge—is presented in the form of a slave narrative that can be read as a model for contemporary readers attempting to engage these brutal realities. Slave narratives emphasize personal quest as a means of "wrest[ing] the black subject out of anonymity, inferiority and brutal disdain." *Beloved* combines the personal quest theme with the collective memory of racial brutality, for although apocalyptic literature features the destiny of the individual and personal salvation, its "overall perspective is still that of the community."

"Rememorying" is what Morrison's characters call it, and it is the central activity in *Beloved*. Because of it the narrative moves constantly back and forth between past and present, mixing time inextricably, as memory escalates its battle against amnesia. The voice of the former slave "above all remembering his ordeal in bondage" can be "the single most impressive feature of a slave narrative." The characters' rememorying in *Beloved* epitomizes the novel's purpose of conjuring up the spirits and experiences of the past and thus ultimately empowering both characters and readers. *Beloved* pairs the stories of a woman and a man, Sethe and Paul D. Sethe's name may be an allusion to Lethe, the spring of forgetfulness in Greek myth. The past that was too painful for either to remember alone can be recovered together: "Her story was bearable because it was his as well." Their stories reveal that the worst brutality they have suffered "is less a single act than the systematic denial of the reality of black lives," the profound humiliation which both know can be worse than death:

> *That anybody white could take your whole self for anything that came to mind. Not just work, kill, or maim you, but dirty you.*

Remembering is part of reversing the "dirtying" process that robbed slaves of self-esteem.

Apocalypse is a more diffuse experience in *Beloved* than traditionally conceived, and it is presented as something which can be survived, not as an event at the end of linear time. In *Beloved* it is an attempt to free African-Americans from guilt and past suffering. What *Beloved* suggests is that while the suffering of the "black and angry dead" is the inescapable psychological legacy of all African-Americans, they can rescue themselves from the trauma of that legacy by directly confronting it and uniting to loosen its fearsome hold. *Beloved*'s redemptive community of women epitomizes the object of salvation in biblical apocalyptic literature: "the creation of a new society."

Thus, like much African-American writing, *Beloved* does not conclude with a climactic moment. "For the black writer, incompletion is a fact of private and public life and the basis for social and cultural hope." The experience of suffering and guilt can begin to be transformed into knowledge, once the trauma is purged, so that the novel leaves the powerful apocalyptic scene of the community's expurgation of Beloved to observe Sethe and Paul D rejoining their stories to each other's. Paul D, who had left upon learning of the murder, must return to Sethe's house to re-establish the intimate connection which will allow them each to find his or her own self and love it. Paul D, despite his inability to feel when he had first arrived at Sethe's, has a deep understanding of the meaning of slavery and freedom, that under slavery "you protected yourself and loved small," but finding freedom means "to get to a place where you could love anything you chose." Linked with Sethe's mother in several ways, including the wearing of the bit, he mothers Sethe as her own mother never could, and when he does, the voice of his lynched best friend enters his mind, speaking about the woman he loved, "She is a friend of my mind. She gather me, man. The pieces I am, she gather them and give them back to me in all the right order."

Beloved is a novel about collecting fragments and welding them into beautiful new wholes, about letting go of pain and guilt, but also recovering what is lost and loving it into life. One of its most poignant images is the ribbon that Stamp Paid finds on the river bottom—"a red ribbon knotted around a curl of wet woolly hair, clinging still to its bit of scalp." Although he knows all the horrors of 1874—the lynchings, whippings, burnings of colored schools, rapes, and lynch fires—it is this discovery which finally weakens Stamp Paid's bone marrow and makes him "dwell on Baby Suggs' wish to consider what in the world was harmless."

What Morrison creates is far from harmless. She knows how painful it is to remember the horrors she presents. She has said in an interview that she expected *Beloved* to be the least read of all her books because "it is about something that the characters don't want to remember, I don't want to remember, black people don't want to remember, white people don't want to remember. I mean, it's national amnesia." However, because Beloved insists on remembering, the novel is able to recover and honor the symbolic spirit of the Black girl whose ribbon and piece of scalp Stamp Paid found. In so doing, it makes possible the contemplation and creation of a future in which African-Americans can respect and honor themselves and their ancestors—be beloved. As Paul D says to Sethe, "Me and you, we got more yesterday than anybody. We need some kind of tomorrow." What *Beloved* suggests is that tomorrow is made possible by the knowledge of yesterday, a knowledge that for contemporary African-Americans can be gained from imagining what it was like to walk in the flesh of their slave ancestors.

> *Auschwitz lies on the other side of life and on the other side of death. There, one lives differently, one walks differently, one dreams differently. . . . Only those who lived it in their flesh and their minds can possibly transform their experience into knowledge.*

By giving its readers the inside view of slaves' lives—which bore uncanny resemblance to the holocaust—the novel enables its African-American readers to live the experience of slavery in their minds and to join in the healing primal sound of the women who come to Sethe's yard. By speaking the horror, Morrison assumes and helps to create the community that can hear and transform it.

—Susan Bowers, "*Beloved* and the New Apocalypse," *The Journal of Ethnic Studies* 18:1 (Spring 1990): pp. 61–63; 73–75.

❖

DAVID LAWRENCE ON EXORCISING GHOSTS FROM BODY AND COMMUNITY IN *BELOVED*

[In this extract, David Lawrence examines the ghostly Beloved as a threat to Sethe and the community that must be exorcised in order to save them both.]

In William Faulkner's *Light in August*, Byron Bunch reflects that no matter how much a person might "talk about how he'd like to escape from living folks . . . it's the dead folks that do him the damage." The damage done by dead folks in Toni Morrison's *Beloved* points to the central position accorded to memory, the place where these dead folks are kept alive, in this novel of futile forgetting and persistent remembrance. Operating independently of the conscious will, memory is shown to be an active, constitutive force that has the power to construct and circumscribe identity, both individual and collective, in the image of its own contents. Sethe's "rememory," in giving substance to her murdered daughter and to the painful past, casts its spell over the entire community, drawing the members of that community into one person's struggle with the torments of a history that refuses to die.

In portraying the capacity of the past to haunt individual and community life in the present, *Beloved* brings into daylight the "ghosts" that are harbored by memory and that hold their "hosts" in thrall, tyrannically dictating thought, emotion, and action. The stories of the tightly woven network of characters culminate in a ritualistic sacrifice of Beloved, a ceremony that frees the community from this pervasive haunting. The supernatural existence of Beloved, who acts as a scapegoat for the evils of the past, threatens the naturalized set of inherited codes by which the community defines itself. The climactic scene shows how a culture may find it necessary in a moment of crisis to exorcise its own demons in order to reaffirm its identity.

Morrison first exposes, however, the workings of the internal mechanisms that have generated the need for exorcism in the first place. A deeply encoded rejection of the body drives the highly pressurized haunting in *Beloved*. The black community of Cincinnati is caught in a cycle of self-denial, a suffocating repression of fundamental bodily needs and wants. The inability to articulate such embodied experience, to find a text for the desiring body within communal codes, obstructs self-knowledge and does violence to the fabric of community. Woven into the dense texture of the novel, into what Morrison has called the "subliminal, the underground life of a novel," the interaction of language and body underlies the collective confrontation with the ghosts of memory. In her representation of this psychic battle, Morrison fashions word and flesh as intimate allies in the project of constructing a domain in which body and spirit may thrive. The exorcism of Beloved, an embodiment of resurgent desire, opens the way to a reworking of the codes that have enforced the silencing of the body's story, making possible a remembering of the cultural heritage that has haunted the characters so destructively. In the end, the communal body seems ready to articulate a reinvigorated language that, in returning to its roots in the body, empowers its speakers to forge a more open, inclusive community.

In a novel that examines the dehumanizing impact of slavery, one might expect that the white man, the monstrous enforcer of slavery's brutality, would haunt the black community. The haunting occurs, however, within a social structure relatively insulated from the white community and, in its most intense form, springs from the "rememory" of an ex-slave in the form of one victimized by slavery. There is nothing mysteriously threatening about whites; on the contrary, "white folks didn't bear speaking on. Everybody knew." Of course, whites "spoke on" their slaves tirelessly, and, in the exploration of political power in the novel, ownership of body and authorship of language are shown to be insidiously linked. Under the regime of white authority, the "blackness" of the slave's body represents for "whitefolks" an animal savagery and moral depravity that, ironically, ends up remaking them in the image of their own fears:

> Whitepeople believed that whatever the manners under every dark skin was a jungle. Swift unnavigable waters, screaming baboons, sleeping snakes, red gums ready for sweet white blood. . . . But it wasn't the jungle blacks brought with them to this place from the other (livable) place. It was the jungle whitefolks planted in them. And it grew. It spread. In, through and after life, it spread, until it invaded the whites who had made it. . . . The screaming baboon lived under their own white skin; the red gums were their own.

This "belief," which underlies the chilling scientific rationality of schoolteacher, abstracts the human corporeality of the slave into a sign for the other in the discourse of the dominant ideology. Further, such invasive signifying upon the black body generates a self-fulfilling prophecy, as blacks find themselves unable to assert an identity outside the expectations imposed upon them: "The more [colored people] used themselves up to persuade whites of something Negroes believed could not be questioned, the deeper and more tangled the jungle grew inside."

In *Beloved*, the question of authority over one's own body is consistently related to that of authority over discourse; bodily and linguistic disempowerment frequently intersect. At Sweet Home, Sethe makes the ink with which schoolteacher and his nephews define on paper her "animal characteristics"; the ink, a tool for communication produced by her own hands, is turned against her as ammunition for their "weapons" of torture, pen and paper. Shocked, she asks Mrs. Garner for the definitions of "characteristics" and "features," vainly attempting to assert control over the words that have conscripted her body in a notebook. The terror she feels at seeing herself defined and divided (animal traits on the left, human on the right) concludes her list on ways whites can "dirty you so bad you forgot who you were"; the litany of brutality—decapitations, burnings, rapes—she provides Beloved as "reasons" for killing her ends with this bottom line: "And no one, nobody on this earth, would list her daughter's characteristics on the animal side of the paper. No. Oh no."

—David Lawrence, "Fleshly Ghosts and Ghostly Flesh: The Word and the Body in Beloved," *Studies in American Fiction* 19:2 (Autumn 1991):189–91.

♣

BERNARD BELL ON MORRISON'S WOMANIST REMEMBRANCES OF THINGS PAST

[Bernard W. Bell is Professor of English at Pennsylvania State University. His most recent volume of criticism is *The Afro-American Novel and Its Tradition* (1987). In this extract, Bell discusses *Beloved* as a postmodern romance about the resilience of African-Americans.]

On a sociopsychological level, *Beloved* is the story of Sethe Suggs's quest for social freedom and psychological wholeness. Sethe struggles with the haunting memory of her slave past and the retribution of Beloved, the ghost of the infant daughter that she killed in order to save her from the living death of slavery. On a legendary and mythic level, *Beloved* is a ghost story that frames embedded narratives of the impact of slavery, racism, and sexism on the capacity for love, faith, and community of black families, especially of black women, during the Reconstruction period. Set in post-Civil-War Cincinnati, *Beloved* is a womanist neo-slave narrative of double consciousness, a postmodern romance that speaks in many compelling voices and on several time levels of the historical rape of black American women and of the resilient spirit of blacks in surviving as a people. . . .

As the author has explained in the interviews and as a sympathetic white minister's report in the February 12, 1856, issue of the *American Baptist* reveals, at the center of *Beloved* is Morrison's retelling of the chilling historical account of a compassionate yet resolute self-emancipated mother's tough love. Margaret Garner, with the tacit sympathy of her sexagenarian mother-in-law, cut the throat of one of her four children and tried to kill the others to save them from the outrages of slavery that she had suffered. Guided by the spirits of the many thousands gone, as inscribed in her dedication, Morrison employs a multivocal text and a highly figurative language to probe her characters' double consciousness of their terribly paradoxical circumstances as people and non-people in a social arena of white male hegemony. She also foregrounds infanticide as a desperate act of "'thick'" love by a fugitive-slave mother "with iron eyes and backbone to match."

"'Love is or it ain't,'" Sethe, the dramatized narrator/protagonist, says in reproach to a shocked fried, Paul D. "'Thin love ain't love at all.'" Indignantly reflecting on Paul D's metonymic reprimand that she "'got two feet . . . not four,'" she later expands on their oppositional metaphors in reverie: "Too thick, he said. My love was too thick. What he know about it? Who in the world is he willing to die for? Would he give his privates to a stranger in return for a carving?"

The implied author, the version of herself that Morrison creates as she creates the narrative, brilliantly dramatizes the moral, sexual, and epistemological distances between Sethe and Paul D. After their first dialogue, a trackless, quiet forest abruptly appears between them. This metaphorical silence is an ingenious, ironic use of the techniques of call and response that invites the implied reader—in Wolfgang Iser's words, that "network of response-inviting structures, which impel the reader to grasp the text"—to pause and take stock of his or her own ambivalent moral and visceral responses to this slave mother's voicing of her thick love.

Thematically, the implied author interweaves racial and sexual consciousness in *Beloved*. Sethe's black awareness and rejection of white perceptions and inscriptions of herself, her children, and other slaves as non-human—marking them by letter, law, and lash as both animals and property—are synthesized with her black feminist sense of self-sufficiency. Sethe reconciles gender differences with first her husband Halle Suggs, and later Paul D, in heterosexual, endogamous relationships that affirm the natural and Biblical principles of the racial and ethnic survival of peoplehood through procreation and parenting in extended families. Although the implied author blends racial and sexual consciousness, the structure and style of the text foreground the ambivalence of slave women about motherhood that violates their personal integrity and that of their family.

Foregrounding the theme of motherhood, Morrison divides the text into twenty-eight unnumbered mini-sections, the usual number of days in a woman's monthly menstrual cycle, within three larger, disproportionate sections. Within these sections, Sethe experiences twenty-eight happy days of "having women friends, a mother-in-law, and all of her children together; of being part of a neighborhood; of, in fact, having neighbors at all to call her own." Also within these sections, the passion and power of memory ebb and flow in a discontinuous, multivocal discourse of the present with the past. Unlike the univocal, nineteenth-century slave narratives, in which plot rides character in the protagonist's journey of transformation from object to subject, *Beloved* is a haunting story of a mother's love that frames a series of interrelated love stories (maternal, parental, filial, sororal, conjugal, heterosexual, familial, and communal) by multiple narrators. These stories begin in 1873 and end in 1874, but flash back intermittently to 1855. In the flashbacks and reveries, the omniscient narrator invokes ancestral black women's remembrances of the terror and horror of the Middle Passage. She also probes the deep physical and psychic wounds of Southern slavery, especially the paradoxes and perversities of life on Sweet Home plantation in Kentucky, and recalls Sethe's bold flight to freedom in Ohio in 1855. Freedom, as Paul D's and Sethe's stories most dramatically illustrate, is to get to a place where you could love anything you chose—not to need permission for desire.

—Bernard W. Bell, "*Beloved:* A Womanist Neo-Slave Narrative; or Multivocal Remembrances of Things Past," *African American Review* 26:1 (Spring 1992): 8–10.

❖

STEPHANIE A. DEMETRAKOPOULOS ON THE DEATH OF THE MATERNAL IN SETHE

[Stephanie A. Demetrakopoulos teaches at Western Michigan University and has written extensively on the interrelationship of psychology and spirituality in literature. She is co-editor of *New Dimensions of Spirituality: A Biracial and Bicultural Reading of the Novels of Toni Morrison* (1987) and author of *Listening to Our Bodies: The Rebirth of Feminine Wisdom* (1983). In this extract, Demetrakopoulos examines motherhood in *Beloved;* Baby Suggs and Sethe as women defined by maternal bonds and the cruelties of slavery.]

Beloved is, on an historical and sociological level, a Holocaust book, and like much Holocaust literature, it marvels at the indifferent and enduring beauty of nature as a frame for the worst human atrocities. This theme is central to *And the Sun Kept On Shining,* for example, in which the author loses her entire family and then is stripped of her humanity in a Nazi death camp. Similarly, in both Alain Resnais' *Night and Fog* and his recent *Shoah,* the camera lingers ironically on beautiful landscapes as a voice-over comments on the pastoral setting where Jews were slaughtered and buried in mass graves. In Morrison's novel, Sethe marvels at how the beautiful landscape of Sweet Home recurs more often in her memories as a pastoral vision than as the slaughterhouse it finally became. Nature erases atrocities, but this allows humans to repeat them.

The originality of *Beloved* lies in Morrison's delineation of the cruelty of the nature *within.* Her use of the pathetic fallacy ironically underlines the cruel absurdity of maternal passion. After Sethe gives birth to Denver, Morrison comments on the lie of fecundity in their environment. The spores of bluefern floating in the river, she writes,

> are seeds in which the whole generation sleeps confident of a future. And for a moment it is easy to believe that each one has one—will become all of what is contained in the spore: will live out its days as planned. This moment of certainty lasts no longer than that; longer, perhaps than the spore itself.

But tenuous, frail, as almost certainly doomed as newborn life is, the mother instinct takes upon itself total and crushing responsibility for the fruition of its offspring. Sethe repeatedly cites her milk as a kind of panacea, even as the bonding element of her family.

To fully understand the extent to which Sethe's maternal bonds almost destroy her, we must look closely at the life stages that her surviving daughter Denver passes through. Denver's round, brown, chubby body symbolizes the *gravitas* of social reality, of history, which she so prosaically embodies. This is the same prosaic quality suggested by Denver's name, her typically little-girl secret room in the bushes, and her adolescent response to Paul D's entering her mother's life (Denver is both waiting for her father Halle and embarrassed by her mother's sexuality). Like Nel in *Sula* and Hagar in *Song of Solomon*, Denver needs community and family, traditional ties. She is the female survivor in Western culture, the hardheaded practical one who will finally seek work and make connections with the outside world. We see this early in her discovery of Lady Jones's classes; we see her heading for a future in American culture and society at the close of the novel as a young man pursues her down the street; and we have earlier been told that perhaps she will go to Oberlin College. Denver, in short, comes to embody the history that Sethe so resists entering.

In an awesomely strong manner, Denver finally gives birth to her Self, her own Identity. Her mother has ensured Denver's life, her survival; but Sethe has not projected futures for Denver that might ensure the child's ability to step into womanhood. Denver's consciousness as a female emerges for her as she sits alone in her bower (a word that has resonated with sexual connotations since Milton and Spenser's use of bowers as symbols for prelapsarian female sexuality), and her emergent adolescent sexuality is part of what impels her identification with Beloved, who unwittingly provides one step toward maturity for Denver's Womanself, struggling to be born. Part of Denver's strength lies in her genetic heritage: When she goes to look for work, we are told that she is her father's daughter. And Paul D remarks at the conclusion of the novel on how much she looks like Halle, who offers a superb image of male nurturing, industry, and compassion. Coupled with Sethe's strength, the qualities associated with Halle will, we know, carry Denver far.

Denver actually midwives two female souls into the toils of adult individuation—her mother Sethe's as well as her own. Denver helps deliver Sethe from her deadly bond with Beloved. It is from Denver that Sethe takes the word *plans* and by the end of the book is able to apply this concept to herself. Denver uses whatever raw material she finds around her to help her out of the matriarchal cave into life. Even Beloved serves as a foothold, a rung on the ladder; as a woman one step ahead in sexual development. Also, in mothering Beloved, Denver remothers herself away from her fears of Sethe, which began when she accidentally learned of her sister's murder. When Denver tells Sethe's story to Beloved, she really *knows* it for the first time; it becomes far more than just words, the myth of her own origin. She begins to understand how her mother suffered and finally becomes protective of Sethe as she sees the actual flesh of Sethe disappearing in the devouring bond with Beloved. Denver is realistic enough to see that something must be done, and it is through her agency that the community of women mobilize to exorcise Beloved. Sethe is tied only to her past, whereas Denver is interested only in the present until she matures to become the caretaker of her caretaker and enters the future. For a time, Denver must precociously become Demeter, until Paul D returns to catalyze Sethe out of her sickbed. The live daughter as rescuer supplants the dead daughter as succubus. Sethe's girl child does finally mean her life.

> —Stephanie A. Demetrakopoulos, "Maternal Bonds as Devourers of Women's Individuation in Toni Morrison's *Beloved*," *African American Review* 26:1 (Spring 1992): 54–56.

❖

LINDA KRUMHOLZ ON BELOVED AS A STORY OF INDIVIDUAL AND NATIONAL REMEMORY

[Linda Krumholz has recently taught American literature as a Visiting Assistant Professor at Oberlin College. In this extract, Krumholz discusses *Beloved* as Morrison's reconceptualization of American history.]

Morrison uses ritual as a model for the healing process. Rituals function as formal events in which symbolic representations—such as dance, song, story, and other activities—are spiritually and communally endowed with the power to shape real relations in the world. In *Beloved*, ritual processes also imply particular notions of pedagogy and epistemology in which—by way of contrast with dominant Western traditions—knowledge is multiple, context-dependent, collectively asserted, and spiritually derived. Through her assertion of the transformative power of ritual and the incorporation of rituals of healing into her narrative, Morrison invests the novel with the potential to construct and transform individual consciousness as well as social relations.

To make the novel work as a ritual, Morrison adapts techniques from Modernist novels, such as the fragmentation of the plot and a shifting narrative voice, to compel the reader to actively construct an interpretive framework. In *Beloved* the reader's process of reconstructing the fragmented story parallels Sethe's psychological recovery: Repressed fragments of the (fictionalized) personal and historical past are retrieved and reconstructed. Morrison also introduces oral narrative techniques—repetition, the blending of voices, a shifting narrative voice, and an episodic framework—that help to simulate the aural, participatory dynamics of ritual within the private, introspective form of the novel. In many oral traditions, storytelling and poetry are inseparable from ritual, since words as sounds are perceived as more than concepts; they are events with consequences. Morrison uses Modernist and oral techniques in conjunction with specifically African-American cultural referents, both historical and symbolic, to create a distinctly African-American voice and vision which, as in Baby Sugg's rituals, invoke the spiritual and imaginative power to teach and to heal.

The central ritual of healing—Sethe's "rememory" of and confrontation with her past—and the reader's ritual of healing correspond to the three sections of the novel. In part one the arrival first of Paul D then of Beloved forces Sethe to confront her past in her incompatible roles as a slave and as a mother. Moving from the fall of 1873 to the winter, the second part describes Sethe's period of atonement, during which she is enveloped by the past, isolated in her house with Beloved, who forces her to suffer over and over again all the pain and shame of the past. Finally, part three is Sethe's ritual "cleaning," in which the women of the community aid her in casting out the voracious Beloved, and Sethe experiences a repetition of her scene of trauma with a difference—this time she aims her murderous hand at the white man who threatens her child.

The three phases of the reader's ritual also involve a personal reckoning with the history of slavery. In part one, stories of slavery are accumulated through fragmented recollections, culminating in the revelation of Sethe's murder of her child in the last chapters of the section. In part two, the reader is immersed in the voices of despair. Morrison presents the internal voices of Sethe, Denver, and Beloved in a ritual chant of possession, while Paul D and Stamp Paid are also overwhelmed by the legacy of slavery. The last part of the novel is the reader's "clearing," achieved through the comic relief of the conversation of Paul D and Stamp Paid and the hopeful reunion of Sethe and Paul D. The novel concludes with Denver's emergence as the new teacher, providing the reader with a model for a new pedagogy and the opportunity for the reconstruction of slave history from a black woman's perspective.

Finally, while *Beloved* can be read as a ritual of healing, there is also an element of disruption and unease in the novel, embodied in the character of Beloved. As an eruption of the past and the repressed unconscious, Beloved catalyzes the healing process for the characters and for the reader; thus, she is a disruption necessary for healing. But Beloved also acts as a trickster figure who defies narrative closure or categorization, foreclosing the possibility of a complete "clearing" for the reader. Thus, as the reader leaves the book, we have taken on slavery's haunt as our own.

—Linda Krumholz, "The Ghosts of Slavery: Historical Recovery in Toni Morrison's *Beloved*," *African American Review* 26:3 (Fall 1992): 396–397.

❖

Elizabeth Fox-Genovese on the Story That Could Not Be Passed On

[Elizabeth Fox-Genovese is Eleonore Raoul Professor of the Humanities and Professor of History at Emory University. Among her published works are *Feminism Without Illusions: A Critique of Individualism* (1991), *Within the Plantation Household: Black and White Women of the Old South* (1988), and, with Eugene Genovese, *Fruits of Merchant Capital: Slavery and Bourgeois Property in the Rise and Expansion of Capitalism* (1983). In this extract, Fox-Genovese asks, "Was slavery an external force or an internal presence?" and proposes alternative readings of Sethe's infanticide.]

For Sethe, Beloved is the daughter who has come back to her. "She mine. See. She come back to me of her own free will and I don't have to explain a thing." Beloved is the child to whom she can tell of Sweet Home, to whom she can talk of the things that Denver does not want to hear. For Denver Beloved, "is my sister. I swallowed her blood right along with my mother's milk. . . . Ever since I was little she was my company and she helped me wait for my daddy." Denver loves her mother, but knows "she killed because of it." Denver knows that there is something in her mother "that makes it all right to kill her own." And she constantly fears that "the thing that happened that made it all right for my mother to kill my sister could happen again." Denver does not know and does not want to know what that thing might be. She only knows that it comes from outside 124, and so she never leaves the house, carefully watching over the years "so it can't happen again and my mother won't have to kill me too." More frightening yet, maybe "the thing that makes it all right to kill her children" is still in her mother.

The ghost of the victim—the name on the tombstone of the victim—of an infanticide prompted by too-thick love, Beloved is the custodian of the story that was not to be passed on. Her arrival at 124 signals her refusal to lay it down and get on with things. Nothing can be laid down or got on with until the story is told. The story belongs to no one person but to them all—the folks from Sweet Home who made it to 124. Baby Suggs feared that the murder had occurred because of the Sweet Home escapees' too great arrogance about their freedom. Twenty days after Sethe's safe arrival, Baby Suggs had given a party for ninety people who "ate so well, and laughed so much, it made them angry." So when they awoke the next morning the odor of their disapproval at what they took to be Baby Suggs' over-stepping hung in the air, masking the odor of the "dark and coming thing" that was the four horsemen in pursuit of Sethe. Had it not been for the party, Baby Suggs worried, might they not have recognized the threat soon enough to take steps to avert it?

Baby Suggs' worries link Sethe's infanticide to the free black community. Sethe's and Paul D's memories link it to Sweet Home and, beyond Sweet Home, to slavery as a social system. For Paul D fully corroborates Sethe's fragmented account of life at Sweet Home, demonstrating that we should not mistrust her memories. It was that bad. In fact, under Schoolteacher, it was so bad as to cast doubt upon their belief that it had really been any better under the Garners. The issue is not a good or a bad master. The issue is slavery. And a slavery that leaves the defin-ition of men to the good will of a master, rather than to the identity of the men themselves, is also a slavery that destroys the definition of women—especially mothers. Sethe, having barely known her own mother and lacking the companionship of other women, knew nothing of the practices of mothering. But by the time she arrived at 124, she knew that her very identity depended upon her children's being absolutely hers.

There are strong reasons to accept Sethe's infanticide as a desperate act of self-definition: By claiming her child absolutely, she claimed her identity as a mother, not a breeder. But in grounding her defense of her identity as a mother in the murder of her own child, she opened new possibilities of being viewed as an animal. The responses of Denver and Paul D, like the absence of Howard and Buglar, remind us that Sethe's self-definition was also the "crawling already?" baby's murder. Was it a thing outside or a thing inside that made Sethe do what she did? Was slavery an external force or an internal presence? By giving Beloved a consciousness, however briefly and elliptically, Morrison seems to suggest that we cannot entirely cast the murder of a baby as an act of heroic, if tormented, resistance. By peopling Beloved's consciousness with memories that evoke the slave ships of the middle passage, she seems to suggest that we cannot entirely divorce the murder of this baby from the slavery that shaped its murdering mother's life.

—Elizabeth Fox-Genovese "Unspeakable Things Unspoken: Ghosts and Memories in *Beloved*," published as "Unspeakable Things Unspoken: Ghosts and Memories in the Narratives of African-American Women" from *The 1992 Elsa Goveia Memorial Lecture presented at The University of the West Indies, Mona, Jamaica, 26 March 1992.*

❧

ASHRAF H. D. RUSHDY ON SETHE'S PROCESS OF HEALING

[Ashraf H. D. Rushdy is author of *The Empty Garden: The Subject of Late Milton* (1992). In this extract, Rushdy proposes that Sethe's infanticide is impossible to judge apart from the circumstances of slavery.]

The obvious place to begin a reading tracing Morrison's signifyin(g) on the story of Margaret Garner is the site of infanticide. One of the recurrent tropes of the African American novel of slavery is the possible response to an institution attempting to render meaningless the mother-child relationship. In William Wells Brown's *Clotelle*, the slave mother Isabella would rather commit suicide than face slavery for herself and her children. Hunted by a crowd of dogs and slavecatchers, Isabella leaps into the Potomac as an act symbolizing the "unconquerable love of liberty which the human heart may inherit." The chapter is entitled "Death Is Freedom." In Zora Neale Hurston's *Moses, Man of the Mountain*, slavery is described as an institution in which only death can give freedom. As Amram tells Caleb, "you are up against a hard game when you got to die to beat it." It is an even harder game, Morrison would add, when you have to kill what you love most.

Coffin explicitly states Margaret's motivation: "the slave mother . . . killed her child rather than see it taken back to slavery." Like Harriet Jacobs, Margaret, in Coffin's reading of her history, sees death as a better alternative than slavery. "It seemed to me," writes Jacobs, "that I would rather see them [her children] killed than have them given up to his [the slave-owner's] power . . .When I lay down beside my child, I felt how much easier it would be to see her die than to see her master beat her about."

Sethe killed Beloved, according to Stamp Paid, because she "was trying to outhurt the hurters." "She love those children." Loving as a slave, according to Paul D (whom Stamp Paid is trying to persuade with his assessment of Sethe's motivation), meant loving small, loving in an unobvious way so that whatever was loved did not become part of a technique of punishment. Paul D's advice, and his credo, was to "love just a little bit" so that when the slave owners took whatever or whoever the slave loved and "broke its back, or shoved it in a croaker sack, well, maybe you'd have a little love left over for the next one." Ella, another ex-slave who was loved by no one and who considered "love a serious disability," lived by the simple dictum "Don't love nothing." When Paul D learns of Sethe's infanticide he tells her that her love is "too thick." She responds by telling him that "Love is or it ain't. Thin love ain't love at all." Although Paul D lives by his philosophy of loving small as a protective measure, he knows what Sethe means. "He knew exactly what she meant: to get to a place where you could love anything you chose—not to need permission for desire—well now, *that* was freedom." Although Paul D knows the conditions of freedom and Sethe knows the conditions of love, each has to learn to claim that freedom, to claim that love, and thereby to claim genuine community and begin the process of healing.

Sethe's process of healing occurs when she acknowledges her act and accepts her responsibility for it while also recognizing the reason for her act within a framework larger than that of individual resolve. Here, perhaps, is Morrison's most powerful introjection into the Margaret Garner story—the establishing of a context for Sethe's act. Sethe's own mother kills all the children fathered by the whites who raped her. As Nan, Sethe's grandmother tells her, "She threw them all away but you. The one from the crew she threw away on the island. The others from more whites she also threw away. Without names, she threw them." Another important person helping Sethe through the exorcising of her painful memories is Ella, who, it is hinted, has also committed infanticide. By placing such a frame around Sethe's story, Morrison insists on the impossibility of judging an action without reference to the terms of its enactment—the wrongness of assuming a transhistorical ethic outside a particular historical moment. Morrison is not justifying Sethe's actions; she is writing about them in the only way she knows how—through eyes that accuse and embrace, through a perspective that criticizes while it rejoices. Towards that end, she has constructed two daughterly presences in her novel who help Sethe remember and forget her personal history, who embody the dual perspective of critique and rejoicing.

Beloved, the incarnation of the ghost of the murdered daughter, is the most obvious revisionist construction in Morrison's novel. Through Beloved, she signifies on history by resurrecting one of its anonymous victims. When Beloved comes back to haunt Sethe for murdering her, Beloved becomes the incarnated memory of Sethe's guilt. Moreover, she is nothing but guilt, a symbol of an unrelenting criticism of the dehumanizing function of the institution of slavery. In this, she is the daughter representing a severe critique, demonstrating the determinism in slave history. She represents, however, only half of Morrison's work: the accusing glare, the unforgiving perspective, the need to forget—"It was not a story to pass on." There is another daughter in the novel, another daughter of history—representing the embracing glance, the loving view, the need to remember.

When Sethe first sees the reincarnated Beloved, her "bladder filled to capacity." She runs immediately to the outhouse, but does not make it: "Right in front of its door she had to lift her skirts, and the water she voided was endless. Like a horse, she thought, but as it went on and on she thought, No, more like flooding the boat when Denver was born. So much water Amy said, 'Hold on, Lu. You going to sink us you keep that up.' But there was no stopping water breaking from a breaking womb and there was no stopping now." She would later, in a retrospective moment, remember this scene in trying to discover who Beloved could be. What is worth noticing, though, is that at that precise moment she does not remember the birth of Beloved but the birth of Denver. Denver is the fictional recreation of Margaret Garner's other daughter, the daughter who survives. Coffin describes Garner and this daughter in the courtroom: "The babe she held in her arms was a little girl, about nine months old, and was much lighter in color than herself, light enough to show a red tinge in its cheek." In *Beloved,* Denver becomes the daughter of hope.

—Ashraf H. D. Rushdy "Daughters Signifyin(g) History: The Example of Toni Morrison's *Beloved," American Literature* 64:3 (September 1992): 576–578.

❖

Josef Pesch on *Beloved* as a Novel in the American Apocalyptic Tradition

[In this extract, Josef Pesch examines Sethe's "conflict of forgetting and remembering" as post-apocalyptic narrative, focused not on the future, but on the past.]

Although based on fact, *Beloved* presents a fictional view. Objective facts, a mother becoming a killer, murdering her own child, are there, but the reality of the fiction takes us beyond those facts, makes us partake in her struggles to come to grips with her deed and her attempts at finding a *modus vivendi* in the post-apocalyptic work of art which takes us beyond itself into a realm of timeless being where Beloved, killed, dead, and buried, comes alive as a rememory all readers share, alive forever in their minds, calling them to contemplation, removing them—particularly in its final pages—from reality, its political pressures for apportioning blame and calls for action, thus allowing them to let the rememory get to them where they might be repressing it or otherwise looking elsewhere, enabling them to acknowledge what has happened, to share the experience from the inside.

The baby is dead and nothing can change this. The apocalypse has happened and cannot be reversed, but Beloved remains, turned into *Beloved,* i.e., aesthetic knowledge, into a rememory which, though painful, will never be forgotten. She has become music, a symphony in words, our thought picture, rendering this fictional reality intensely ours. The aesthetic knowledge recorded here is beyond delivering simple messages of hope or doom; as post-apocalyptic art it makes us partake in a complex vision.

The breaking down of boundaries, the striving for an openness characteristic of modern works of art—as Eco defines it —is also reflected in the closure of *Beloved.* The "climax" for which the novel seems to be heading—the second coming—is not its end: "*Beloved* does not conclude with a climactic moment." This ending is rejected when Denver stops Sethe's attack on Bodwin. *Beloved* has a happy ending, in which Paul D. joins Sethe in her reclamation of self: "'Me? Me?'" and again the book could have ended there. It does not, as it represents an ongoing post-apocalyptic work of art that is larger than Sethe's or Paul D.'s stories. The novel's central "character" never dies. As *BELOVED* she is present before the novel begins, engraved on the novel's cover; as "Beloved" she remains imprinted outside the story as the novel's final word.

Beloved has no end and the memory of Beloved cannot be exorcized. Her disembodied voice appears again in the post-narration on the final pages full of paradox: "Disremembered and unaccounted for, she cannot be lost because no one is looking for her," yet she finally asserts herself in print. Thus, here is the essence of *Beloved*: Forget and remember; the necessity of forgetting all too painful "rememory"; the painful impossibility to forget; the necessity to remember in order to build up a fund of knowledge to improve on the reaction to threats to one's life; and the potential uselessness of this knowledge in different, if similar, situations.

"There is no hope in this," as Paul Auster pointed out in a different context, "but neither is there despair." "Postmodernism [as] an art of erosion" has post-apocalyptically eroded both. Although post-apocalypse, at least you know there is a chance of survival: "it will remember itself from every sides." Thus the rest is definitely not silence, but—as the novel has it on its concluding page: "weather." Everything is moving, everything is changing; and small butterflies may cause (unpredictably) large effects, cycling and recycling. To exorcise Beloved would be attempting to erase her completely, thus remembering by trying to forget. In whatever shape or form, she will always be part of the system (like any impulse remains in the weather system). No matter how minute the power of that memory will be, under the "right" circumstances effects may again be devastating. "Power was everywhere," but one never knows what input will produce which effect—and on what scale—in this highly complex system called humanity. A system, indeed, which is failed time and again by attempts at subjecting it to linear descriptions and systems. Once a deed is done, nothing can ever erase it, effects of apocalypses will never go away. The fact that in a very profound sense there is no end is aesthetically reflected in the closure of Morrison's novel, keeping "disorderly life in its flux against orderly death in its finality." *Beloved* closes its own cycle, composing a work of "Beauty out of discord," resting self-content. If "a *knowing* blankness results" (my emphasis), that is something, after all.

—Josef Pesch, "*Beloved:* Toni Morrison's Post-Apocalyptic Novel," *Canadian Review of Comparative Literature* 20:3–4 (September–December 1993): 405–406. ❧

Caroline Rody on *Beloved* as an Historical Novel

[In this extract, Caroline Rody notes how Denver, the inheritor of the story, will take Sethe's family exodus saga into the larger American culture.]

In the "village" of *Beloved*, the multigenerational, culture-bearing black community of Morrison's ideal appears in devastated form, in the persons of a few traumatized survivors, eking out an existence in the aftermath of slavery. Foregrounded in the novel, the telling of stories becomes memory's struggle with catastrophe and loss. For Morrison's characters, as for the novel in its contemporary moment, cultural transmission requires the retrieval of traumatic memories. This "history" thus acquires the function of communal "talking cure": its characters, author, and readers delve into the past, repeating painful stories to work toward the health of fuller awareness.

Beloved opens upon the haunted house where, shunned by the neighborhood, Morrison's heroine Sethe is raising her daughter Denver in an atmosphere of stagnant grief. Together they have come to accept what drove two sons away from home: the "spiteful" baby ghost who makes hand prints in the cake. Into this scene walks Paul D, that rare "kind of man who could walk into a house and make the women cry." His arrival changes the climate of repression: he chases the invisible haunter from the house and sparks in Sethe "the temptation to trust and remember," "to go ahead and feel," for the first time in years. His past, too, has required profound repression: he has a "tobacco tin buried in his chest where a red heart used to be. Its lid rusted shut." Together, Sethe and Paul D begin a mutual talking cure that promises a mutual future. As their halting, gradual storytelling is taken up by other characters, the novel's present unfolds entwined in multiple strands of time, voice, incident, and perspective.

Storytelling becomes the text's self-conscious task; many scenes present a character narrating his or her life to a listener. The novel's distinctive tone arises from the very difficulty of telling for those recovering from the traumas of slavery—witnessing the murder, torture, or sale of family and friends; being whipped, chained, led with an iron bit in the mouth, and housed in an underground "box"; being examined and catalogued in terms of "human" and "animal" characteristics, or forcibly "nursed" by white boys when one's breasts held milk for a baby. These experiences fragment and block the memories of Morrison's ex-slaves, whose stories are revealed in bits, out of sequence, in a painful eking out and holding back often rendered in spare synecdoche: "Paul D had only begun . . . when her fingers on his knee, soft and reassuring, stopped him. . . . Saying more might push them both to a place they couldn't get back from. Sethe rubbed and rubbed. . . . She hoped it calmed him as it did her. Like kneading bread . . . working dough. Nothing better than that to start the day's serious work of beating back the past."

As the narrative loops around events, dramatizing pain's effect on memory, it also suggests a hesitance to force the past out of characters whose memories stand in for the suffering of innumerable unknown people. Any recuperations are performed against a blank background of storylessness, symbolic of our historical knowledge of African Americans and of their representation in our literature. Morrison chooses just one family's haunted house to explicate, but as Grandma Baby Suggs says, "Not a house in the country ain't packed to the rafters with some dead Negro's grief." Every American house is a haunted house. As *Beloved* revives the past in the modes of haunting, memory, and storytelling, it becomes an exercise in the poetics of absence.

Morrison's prose inventively represents the multiple shades of loss and absence known to slaves: "Anybody Baby Suggs knew, let alone loved, who hadn't run off or been hanged, got rented out, loaned out, bought up, brought back, stored up, mortgaged, won, stolen, or seized." Characters tend to gather around them clusters of the lost. "Did Patty lose her lisp?" Baby Suggs wonders about the children sold from her; "what color did Famous' skin finally take?" On his postwar trek north, Paul D saw "twelve dead blacks in the first eighteen miles," and "by the time he got to Mobile, he had seen more dead people than living ones." A traveling man, Paul D brings to the text a voice of tribal griot-cum-historical eyewitness: "During, before, and after the war he had seen Negroes so stunned, or hungry, or tired or bereft it was a wonder they recalled or said anything.

Who, like him, had hidden in caves and fought owls for food . . . stole from pigs . . . slept in trees in the day and walked by night. . . . Once he met a Negro about fourteen years old who lived by himself in the woods and said he couldn't remember living anywhere else. He saw a witless colored woman jailed and hanged for stealing ducks she believed were her own babies. Passages like this bring to the novel cinematic visions of an entire struggling people, among whom Morrison names a precious few characters for detailed narration. The reader learns, like Ella as she aids escaping slaves, to listen "for the holes—the things the fugitives did not say, the questions they did not ask . . . the unnamed, unmentioned people left behind." To demarcate the "holes" Morrison has characters repeat isolated remembered details, metonymies for unre-countable emotional experiences, the more poignant for their banality. Baby Suggs recalls, "My first-born. All I can remember of her is how she loved the burned bottom of bread. Can you beat that? Eight children and that's all I remember."

—Caroline Rody, "Toni Morrison's *Beloved:* History, 'Rememory,' and a 'Clamor for a Kiss,'" *American Literary History* 7:1 (Spring 1995): 99–101.

❖

JAMES BERGER OF THE PLACE OF *BELOVED* IN THE DEBATE ON AMERICAN RACE RELATIONS

[James Berger was a Charles Phelps Taft postdoctoral fellow at the University of Cincinnati, 1996–97, and a visiting assistant professor at George Mason University. He is author of *After the End: Representations of America Post-apocalypse,* portions of which appear in this volume and in *Postmodern Culture* (1995). In this extract, Berger analyzes *Beloved* as an intervention in the American conversation on race and the African American family.]

Events in the United States today make it difficult to agree with readers who claim that the exorcism of Beloved represents a successful working through of America's racial traumas. Indeed, in my view, such optimistic interpretations of *Beloved* participate in the repressions and denials of trauma that the novel opposes. For instance, Ashraf Rushdy holds as exemplary Sethe's friend Ella's repressive attitude toward the past, arguing that by "exorcising Beloved, by not allowing the past to consume the present, [Ella] offers Sethe the opportunity to reclaim herself." Rushdy's statement that "the novel both remembers the victimization of the ex-slaves who are its protagonists and asserts the healing and wholeness that those protagonists carry with them in their communal lives" seems particularly suspect in view of the destructive divisions Morrison portrays in the African American community after Baby Sugg's feast. The community comes together under Ella's leadership to expel the naked, pregnant, and beautiful figure of Beloved, who has perhaps finally become the "flesh" that Baby Suggs urged her congregation to love. While the community, led by Ella, overcomes its divisions and readmits Sethe and Denver, the absent space where Beloved stood is another scar in the symbolic order, sutured by repression. The ritual that can put Beloved to rest must instead resemble Baby Sugg's ceremony in the forest, involving laughing, dancing, and crying. Beloved must, first of all, be mourned.

Some readings render not only the exorcism but even the infanticide unproblematic. Bernard Bell describes *Beloved* as a "retelling of the chilling historical account of a compassionate yet resolute self-emancipated mothers' tough love." This bizarre formulation relates Sethe's act to "the historical rape of black American women and [to] the resilient spirit of blacks in surviving as a people"; both connections are correct, but Bell's interpretation evades what Morrison takes pains not to evade: the traumatic violence within African American communities and the damage to the resilient spirit Bell speaks of.

Bell and Rushdy would agree with Mae Henderson that "the story of oppression becomes a story of liberation; a story of inhumanity has been overwritten as a story of higher humanity." What these and similar interpretations miss, in my view, is that Beloved's story is not over, that the child will return—indeed, has returned. Henderson rightly regards

Sethe's attack on Bodwin during the exorcism as a repetition of the apocalyptic (or, as she puts it, "primal") scene of infanticide. However, Henderson sees Sethe's violence against the white abolitionist as part of a successful working through of the trauma of the infanticide, since Sethe, taking Bodwin for Schoolteacher, believes that she attacks the slave owner and not her daughter. "Thus, by revising her actions," Henderson writes, "Sethe is able to preserve the community, and the community, in turn, is able to protect one of its own."

Bodwin, however, contrary to Henderson's suggestion, is not Schoolteacher. Bodwin is a lifelong and active abolitionist, not an owner of slaves. Sethe, in a state of delusion, mistakes him for Schoolteacher. She sees Bodwin's entrance as portending a reenactment of the apocalyptic scene—that condensation of a multitude of historical traumas—in which her borders were violated by white institutional power and she pushed her daughter through the veil. Henderson's argument raises the question whether there is in fact a hidden connection, recognized by Sethe, between the white abolitionist and the white slave owner. Placing *Beloved* in the context of racial discourse of the 1980s extends the question. Is Sethe's attack on Bodwin an attack also on white liberals? Does Morrison's presentation of Bodwin suggest that, as Kenneth Clark argued in 1964, the white-liberal position on race is a "more insidious" form of racism?

The most prominent evidence for regarding Bodwin as racist is a statuette near the back door of his house of a kneeling black boy, who has an enormous mouth filled with coins for tradesmen and rests on a pedestal bearing the words "At yo Service." While Bodwin despises slavery, he still regards blacks as subservient and has, apparently, no comprehension of African American culture apart from stereotypes. Moreover, during his ride toward his unexpected encounter with Sethe, Morrison shows Bodwin as a vain and self-absorbed man whose chief interest in abolitionism may have been the feelings of moral elevation and political excitement he derived from the movement personally. And Morrison, I believe, links Bodwin here with a view of 1960s liberalism seen from the 1980s. As Bodwin looks back from *twenty years later* to the time of his greatest political and moral achievements, he muses, "Nothing since was as stimulating as the old days of letters, petitions, meetings, debates, recruitment, quarrels, rescue and downright sedition." For Bodwin, as for liberals and leftists in the age of Reaganism, "those heady days were gone now; what remained was the sludge of ill will; dashed hopes and difficulties beyond repair. A tranquil republic? Well, not in this lifetime." Bodwin (like the liberals) senses that his greatest victory, the abolitionist movement (like the civil rights movement), was only a minor triumph in a larger story of defeat. And in both his self-congratulation and his despair, he remains blind to the interests and culture of African Americans, as his facile memory of the murder of Beloved suggests. He recalls "a runaway slavewoman [who] lived in his homestead with her mother-in-law and got herself into a world of trouble. The Society managed to turn infanticide and the cry of savagery around, and build a further case for abolishing slavery. Good years, they were, full of spit and conviction." Good years, that is, for feelings of moral rectitude; terrible years in their content of racial injustice and suffering.

—James Berger, "Ghosts of Liberalism: Morrison's *Beloved* and the Moynihan Report," *PLMA* 111:3 (May 1996): 415–417.

❖

Pamela E. Barnett on Images of Rape and the Super-natural in *Beloved*

[Pamela E. Barnett is visiting assistant professor of English at Emory University. Her articles have appeared in *Women's Studies and Signs*; the essay published in this volume is part of her current, book-length project, *The Language of Rape: Sexual Violence and Late-Twentieth-Century American Narrative*. In this extract, Barnett examines the ways in which Sethe's memories of sexual abuse hold particular power.]

Toni Morrison's *Beloved* is haunted by history, memory, and a specter that embodies both; yet it would be accurate to say that *Beloved* is haunted by the history and memory of rape specifically. While Morrison depicts myriad abuses of slavery like brutal beatings and lynchings, the depictions of and allusions to rape are of primary importance; each in some way helps explain the infanticide that marks the beginnings of Sethe's story as a free woman. Sethe kills her child so that no white man will ever "dirty" her, so that no young man with "mossy teeth" will ever hold the child down and suck her breasts. Of all the memories that haunt Morrison's characters, those that involve sexual abuse and exploitation hold particular power: rape is the trauma that forces Paul D to lock his many painful memories in a "tobacco tin" heart, that Sethe remembers more vividly than the beating that leaves a tree of scars on her back, that destroys Halle's mind, and against which Ella measures all evil.

I say that the book is haunted by rape not to pun idly on the ghostly presence that names the book but to establish the link between haunting and rape that invigorates the novel's dominant trope: the succubus figure. The character Beloved is not just the ghost of Sethe's dead child; she is a succubus, a female demon and nightmare figure that sexually assaults male sleepers and drains them of semen. The succubus figure, which is related to the vampire, another sexualized figure that drains vital fluid, was incorporated into African American folklore in the form of shapeshifting witches who "ride" terrified victims in the night, and Beloved embodies the qualities of that figure as well. In separate assaults, Beloved drains Paul D of semen and Sethe of vitality; symptomatically, Beloved's body swells as she also feeds off her victims' horrible memories of and recurring nightmares about sexual violations that occurred in their enslaved past. But Beloved functions as more than the receptacle of remembered stories; she reenacts sexual violation and thus figures the persistent nightmares common to survivors of trauma. Her insistent manifestation constitutes a challenge for the characters who have survived rapes inflicted while they were enslaved: directly, and finally communally, to confront a past they cannot forget. Indeed, it is apparent forgetting that subjects them to traumatic return; confrontation requires a direct attempt at remembering.

Morrison uses the succubus figure to represent the effects of institutionalized rape under slavery. When the enslaved persons' bodies were violated, their reproductive potential was commodified. The succubus, who rapes and steals semen, is metaphorically linked to such rapes and to the exploitation of African Americans' reproduction. Just as rape was used to dehumanize enslaved persons, the succubus or vampire's assault robs victims of vitality, both physical and psychological. By representing a female rapist figure and a male rape victim, Morrison foregrounds race, rather than gender, as the category determining domination or subjection to rape.

Two memories of rape that figure prominently in the novel echo the succubus's particular form of sexual assault. The narrator refers several times to the incident in which two "mossy-toothed" boys hold Sethe down and suck her breast milk. No less important, Paul D works on a chain gang in Alfred, Georgia, where prisoners are forced to fellate white guards every morning. In addition, Ella is locked up and repeatedly raped by a father and son she calls "the lowest yet," and Stamp Paid's wife, Vashti, is forced into sex by her enslaver. Baby Suggs is compelled to have sex with a straw boss who later breaks his coercive promise not to sell her child and again with an overseer. Sethe's mother is "taken up many times by the crew" during the Middle Passage, as are many other enslaved women. And three women in the novel—Sethe's mother, Baby Suggs, and Ella—refuse to nurse babies conceived through rape. Other allusions to sexual violation include the Sweet Home men's dreams of rape, Sethe's explanation for adopting the mysterious Beloved—her fears that white men will "jump on" a homeless, wandering black girl—and the neighborhood suspicion that Beloved is the black girl rumored to have been imprisoned and sexually enslaved by a local white man who has recently died. There are also acts of desperate prostitution that are akin to rape: Sethe's exchange of sex for the engraving on her baby's tombstone and the Saturday girls' work at the slaughterhouse.

These incidents of rape frame Sethe's explanation for killing her baby daughter. Sethe tries to tell the furious Beloved that death actually protected the baby from the deep despair that killed Baby Suggs, from "what Ella knew, what Stamp saw and what made Paul D tremble": horrific experiences and memories of rape. Whites do "not just work, kill, or maim you, but dirty you," Sethe tells Beloved, "Dirty you so bad you [can't] like yourself anymore.' Sethe passionately insists that she protected her beloved daughter and also herself from "undreamable dreams" in which "a gang of whites invaded her daughter's private parts, soiled her daughter's thighs and threw her daughter out of the wagon." For Sethe, being brutally overworked, maimed, or killed is subordinate to the overarching horror of being raped and "dirtied" by whites; even dying at the hands of one's mother is subordinate to rape.

—Pamela E. Barnett, "Figurations of Rape and the Supernatural in *Beloved*," *PMLA* 112:3 (May 1997): 418–419.

Works by Toni Morrison

The Bluest Eye. 1970.

Sula. 1973.

The Black Book. 1974.

Song of Solomon. 1977.

Tar Baby. 1981.

Dreaming Emmett (play). 1986.

Beloved. 1987.

Jazz. 1992.

Playing in the Dark: Whiteness and the Literary Imagination. 1992.

Birth of a Nation'hood: Gaze, Script, and Spectacle in the O.J. Simpson Case (co-editor with Claudia Brodsky Lacour). 1997.

Paradise. 1998.

Works About
Toni Morrison and *Beloved*

Crouch, Stanley. "Aunt Medea," *New Republic* (October 19, 1987): 38–43.

Davis, Cynthia. "Self, Society and Myth in Toni Morrison's Fiction," *Contemporary Literature* 23:3 (1982): 323–42.

Goldman, Anne E. "'I Made Ink': (Literary) Production and Reproduction in *Dessa Rose* and *Beloved*," *Feminist Studies* 16 (1990): 324.

Henderson, Mae G. "Toni Morrison's *Beloved:* Re-membering the Body as Historical Text," *Comparative American Identities: Race, Sex, and Nationality in the Modern Text.* Hortense J. Spillers, ed. New York: Routledge, 1991. 62–86.

Horvitz, Deborah. "Nameless Ghosts: Possession and Dispossession in Beloved," *Studies in American Fiction* 17 (1989): 157–67.

Keenan, Sally. "'Four Hundred Years of Silence': Myth, History, and Motherhood in Toni Morrison's *Beloved*," *Recasting the World: Writing after Colonialism.* Jonathan White, ed. Baltimore: Johns Hopkins University Press, 1993. 45–81.

Kubitschek, Missy Dehn. *Claiming the Heritage: African-American Women Novelists and History.* Jackson: University Press of Mississippi, 1991. 174, 177.

———. "The Pain of Being Black: An Interview with Toni Morrison," with Bonnie Angelo. *Conversations with Toni Morrison.* Danielle Taylor-Guthrie, ed. Jackson: University Press of Mississippi, 1994. 255–61.

———. "In the Realm of Responsibility: A Conversation with Toni Morrison," with Marsha Jean Darling, *Women's Review of Books* (March 1988): 5–6.

———. "Unspeakable Things Unspoken: The Afro-American Presence in American Literature," *Michigan Quarterly Review* 28 (1989): 32.

Otten, Terry. *The Crime of Innocence in the Fiction of Toni Morrison.* Columbia: University of Missouri Press, 1989. 82–83.

Page, Philip. "Circularity in Toni Morrison's *Beloved,*" *African American Review* 26:1 (Spring 1992): 31–40.

Sale, Maggie. "Call and Response as Critical Method: African-American Oral Traditions and *Beloved,*" *African American Review* 26:1 (Spring 1992): 41–50.

Samuels, Wilfred D., and Clenora Hudson-Weems. "'Ripping the Veil': Meaning through Rememory in *Beloved,*" *Toni Morrison.* Boston: Twayne, 1990. 94–138.

Sitter, Deborah Ayer. "The Making of a Man: Dialogic Meaning in Beloved," *African American Review* 26:1 (Spring 1992): 17–30.

Smith, Valerie. "'Circling the Subject': History and Narrative in *Beloved,*" *Toni Morrison: Critical Perspectives Past and Present.* K.A. Appiah and Henry Louis Gates, Jr., eds. New York: Amistad, 1993. 340–54.

Valade, Roger M., III. "Post Aesthetic Movement," *The Essential Black Literature Guide.* New York: Visible Ink Press, 1996. 299.

Index of
Themes and Ideas